# Contents

# Chapter One

# The Philosophy of the Green Witch

Step into a world where magic and nature are one in the same, where our respect for the earth and its extraordinary expressions of life are held in high regard and celebrated. Welcome, fellow seekers, to the enchanting realm of green witchcraft—an ancient path of wisdom and wonder that invites us all to honor nature in all its powerful splendor.

Whether you're an aspiring green witch, or you're a person who is simply interested in connecting more with nature, and curious about the unique properties of the herbs, essential oils and plants around you, allow this book to assist you in deepening your connection to the natural world around us. In this chapter, you will learn the fundamental philosophy of being a green witch, and what it really takes to be successful in this craft. Prepare yourself for a journey where the powerful energies of nature join with our innermost selves, showcasing the deep bond between this wondrous planet and ourselves.

To start, anyone can be a green witch if you desire and choose to be. It is not a status relegated to women, men or non-binary people alone. Anyone can become a green witch so long as they resonate with the identity and have a profound appreciation for nature, and desire to understand it further. Green witches understand that the planet we live on is not simply unconscious land, and water. Rather, this entire planet is a conscious, living being, and every tree, plant, fruit, vegetable, flower, animal and insect was divinely created and serves an important purpose in maintaining the perfect balance of this realm. To be a green witch is simply to innately understand that this world is our sacred home, brimming with wisdom, energy, and ancient knowledge. To be a green witch is to appreciate that we and nature are not in competition, we are companions.

We understand the profound interconnectedness of all beings, and recognize that we are but one thread woven in the intricate tapestry of life. This realization encourages green witches to cultivate a deep sense of gratitude and responsibility towards the planet and all its inhabitants.

Respect and appreciation lies at the heart of our practice, and it manifests in countless ways. We honor the earth by treading gently upon its surface, walking with mindful steps and leaving no trace of harm in our wake. We seek to live in harmony with nature, embracing sustainable practices that nurture and protect our ecosystems. This may involve anything from adopting an animal in need of a good home from an animal shelter, to adopting eco-friendly habits like recycling, reducing waste, and reusing things where possible. It can mean supporting local, organic agriculture, or creating your own garden. As well, learning about the natural magic present in all the things we often take for granted such as the properties and uses of different plants, herbs, flowers, stones and the

Seasons, and discovering how to safely harness their unique energies in our spell work, potions and recipes to manifest our desires.

Our respect for animals extends beyond mere admiration; it is a deep recognition of their inherent worth and wisdom. We understand that every creature, from the majestic eagle soaring through the sky to the hardworking bees who pollinate most of the crops we consume, contributes to the delicate balance of our world. We seek to live in harmony with our animal companions, treating them with kindness and compassion, and advocating for their well-being. By observing and learning from their behaviors, we tap into a wellspring of instinct and intuition that guides us on our own spiritual journey. This might involve practicing animal communication, studying animal symbolism, and supporting conservation efforts.

If you take nothing else away from this book, please keep in mind that becoming a green witch is not confined to a rigid set of rules or rituals. Instead, it is an ever-evolving path that encourages you to trust your own intuition and embrace your unique energy. There is no right or wrong way to become a green witch or to practice magic—it is a deeply personal experience that flows from the depths of your being. We celebrate diversity and welcome practitioners of all backgrounds and belief systems. Whether you participate in an organized religion or forge your own spiritual path, as long as you honor and revere nature as sacred and blessed, you are walking the green witch's way.

As a newcomer to the green witch path, it is essential to remember that self-reflection and self-care are integral parts of your practice. Take time to connect with nature regularly—go for walks in the woods, sit by a flowing river, or simply spend time in your own backyard, observing the natural world around you. Create a sacred space in your home where you can retreat to find solace and reconnect with the earth's energies. This could be a simple altar adorned with natural objects like stones, a journal for scripting, candles, feathers, or seashells, or a dedicated corner filled with plants and candles. Use this space for meditation, spellwork, or simply to reflect on your experiences and feelings.

One of the beautiful aspects of being a green witch is the emphasis on intuition and personal energy. Trusting your instincts and listening to your inner voice are key to developing a deep connection with nature and harnessing its energies. Allow yourself to explore different forms of divination, such as tarot cards, runes, or scrying, to gain insights and guidance on your path. These tools can serve as bridges between the seen and unseen realms, helping you tap into the wisdom of the earth and the spirits that reside within it.

Remember that green witchcraft is not limited to solitary practice. Seek out like-minded individuals, whether in person or online, to connect and share experiences. Join local nature groups, attend workshops, or participate in community gardening projects. Engaging with others who share your passion for nature and magic can provide inspiration, support, and a sense of belonging.

While there are no specific rules or rituals that a green witch must follow, there are numerous practices you can incorporate into your daily life. Take the time to learn about the magical properties of plants and incorporate them into your cooking, create natural beauty and skincare products, or infuse your space with the aromas of herbal sachets and incense. Explore the art of foraging for wild edibles and medicinal plants in a sustainable and respectful manner. By integrating these practices into your everyday life, you deepen your connection with the natural world and infuse your everyday life with powerful and enchanting magic.

As you start on this path, remember that your journey is a constant process of growth and learning. Be open to new experiences and knowledge, and be patient with yourself as you develop your skills, abilities and understanding. The cycles of nature provide a constant source of inspiration and guidance, reminding us that change is natural and necessary. Embrace the ebb and flow of your own spiritual journey, allowing yourself to evolve and adapt as you connect more deeply with the energies of the earth.

Above all, remember to approach your green witchcraft with curiosity, reverence, and a deep sense of love for the earth and all its creatures. May your path as a green witch be one of profound connection, magic, and growth.

# Chapter Two

# Unveiling the Rich Tapestry of Green Witch History

Magic is not something that only exists in the fictional realm of movies and TV shows. Rather, "magic" is just a word to describe the natural energy present in all things, in the world around you; energy that you can learn to tap into just as the medicine women, medicine men, priests, priestesses and healers of the past did.

Throughout history, green witchcraft has flourished in its diversity worldwide. Across Africa's sun-drenched, rich lands, magical people - shamans, sangomas, and herbalists of all kinds - used their profound knowledge of herbs, natural medicine, and the spirit to nurture deep connections to the land. Through potions, teas and tinctures, they assisted those physical and spiritual transformations. The lineage of the green witch, rooted in African wisdom, cherished the sacredness of nature and the power of ancestral knowledge.

It's difficult to pinpoint exactly who the first green witch in history was, nor who was the first person to use herbs, plants and flowers for magical purposes in recorded history, because so much of human history has been purposely destroyed or hidden from the masses. But, what we know for certain is that green witchcraft dates back tens of thousands of years, and emerged in several cultures around the world. Green witchcraft practices and traditions can be found throughout ancient civilizations and indigenous cultures across different continents from Asia to Europe, and Africa to the Americas.

The closest we might have to the first "green witchcraft book" can be found in Ancient Egypt; it is here that one of the oldest and most important medical texts in history was made. It's known as The Ebers Papyrus, a text that dates back to c.1550 BCE. This text documents various medicinal herbs and the many ailments which they treat. One of the first green witches may have been Imhotep, an ancient Egyptian figure who lived around 2600 BCE. He was the chief advisor of Pharaoh Djoser, and is accredited as the architect of the Step Pyramid of Saqqara. But Imhotep is most famous for his powerful medical expertise, healing others using food and plant medicine. In fact, he is deemed the original "Father of Medicine," because he was a renowned healer and doctor. It is from him that we get the famous phrase, "Let thy food be thy medicine and thy medicine be thy food."

Imhotep's contributions to medicine and healing in ancient Egypt were so unmatched that he was deified and worshiped as a god of medicine. While specific details about his practices and methods are not well-known, historical texts suggest that he was highly knowledgeable about the medicinal properties of plants, food and herbs. He used them and other natural substances to treat various ailments, using his holistic approach to healthcare to care for one's physical and spiritual well-being. Imhotep's legacy as a healer and his association with early advancements in medicine make him a significant figure in the history of herbal magic and healing. Even if he is not officially the very first person in history to use natural magic, his influence and expertise certainly played a crucial role in inspiring future generations of healers.

Similarly, herbal medicine has been practiced in China for at least the past 2,000 years. In fact, in ancient China, a famous text called "Shennong Ben Cao Jing" was created, which detailed hundreds of herbs and their medicinal associations. It was said that they were discovered by the "Divine Farmer" Jiang Shinian, who was the first Yan Emperor, who became a deity amongst Chinese and Vietnamese people.

In the misty landscapes of Europe, green witches emerged alongside the rise and fall of empires. Back then they were known as cunning folk, wise women and wise men, and they mastered herbal remedies and healing practices through divination, and nature-based magic. They crafted potions, charms and communicated with the spirits of plants, animals, and the land itself.

Hildegard von Bingen (born 1098-1179) was a German Benedictine abbess of the medieval period who was celebrated and respected for her deep knowledge of herbal remedies. She recorded her findings in a book called "Physica," where she stressed how nature, particularly plants, can be used to improve our physical well-being.

Agnodice of the 4th century BCE was a remarkable woman who became one of the first women to practice herbal magic in ancient Greece. She worked in Athens as the first female physician and midwife. The high mortality rates of infants and mothers during childbirth compelled her to better understand women's health, and inspired her to focus on women's diseases and gynecology, using natural cures and herbs to heal female patients. She was very successful, but was forced to disguise herself as a man in order to practice medicine, since women were banned from practicing at the time. As her popularity among female patients grew due to her effective treatments, rival physicians falsely accused her of seducing her female patients. She was tried in court, where she revealed herself to be a woman. The women defended her and praised her good work, and so Agnodice was not only acquitted, but the law banning women from practicing medicine was removed.

Overtime, many herbalists and green witches faced persecution and oppression at the hands of corrupt governments and religious organizations. Still, their love for the earth persisted and they secretly passed down what remained of their knowledge throughout generations.

Indigenous cultures worldwide have long utilized plants for their healing properties, with traditional healers passing down knowledge and practices through countless generations. These healers, often regarded as wise women, wise men, or shamans, deeply understood the local flora and their medicinal applications. Their expertise encompassed not only physical healing but also spiritual and emotional well-being.

Caribbean islands also nurtured their own lineage of green witches thanks to the combination of African, Indigenous, and European traditions like obeah, vodou and folk magic. They formed a connection to the land, trees, rivers, and mountains through rituals, divination, spell crafting, and healing practices through their magical arts known as obeah, vodou, and folk magic. In places like Jamaica, during wartime, Obeah practitioners, who were known to possess extensive knowledge of herbal remedies and spiritual rituals, would use plants, roots, and potions to heal the sick and wounded. Becoming guardians of secrets of earth magic, they could shape spells for protection, blessing, and transformation.

Our world has since entered a new era full of different values, belief systems, religions, cultures and views. This has led to a spike in people seeking ancient truth and empowerment through mystical means, who have taken it upon themselves to relearn the magic our ancestors were so familiar with. And, while we may not be able to identify a specific individual as the very first to use herbal medicine for healing, it is clear that the use of plants for medicinal purposes has been an integral part of human history since ancient times. The collective wisdom and experiences of countless individuals across cultures have contributed to the development and refinement of herbal medicine as we know it today.

The concept of the "green witch" occupies a place at the junction of both tradition and progress. Now, more than ever before, people of all genders and races, living in various parts of the globe are embracing this mantle. Modern spiritualists, root workers, and earth lovers of all kinds are meshing old wisdom with fresh perspectives as they take on their journeys into green witchery. It's truly a story woven by us all; every person adds their own thread to create a vivid tapestry full of enchantment, reverence, and an intertwined relationship with natural environments.

So if you're reading these words right now, you are likely an aspiring green witch, a herbalist in training, or a seeker of natural magic! Let us pay homage to all the authentic, kind, brave, and powerful green witches who have gone before – may we remember both the incredible and enchanting women but also the impressive and much-needed males and non-binary individuals for their part in crafting this trail – so that we can all come together in unity and continue weaving the ongoing tale of green witchcraft.

# Chapter Three

# The Power of Nature's Energy and the Green Witch

Have you ever felt a surge of power pass through you on a windy day? Felt an immediate sense of peace while walking through a sun-dappled forest? Or sensed an invisible force as you stood, looking out across a glistening lake, watching the rushing waters pass you by? These are the whispers of energy—the life force that flows through all living beings and nature itself.

Welcome to the realm of energy, where green witches discover a profound source of magic. At the core of our practice, green witches recognize that everything in existence is interconnected by a vibrant energy that ebbs and flows. This understanding guides us to work with the natural powers of the earth, plants, animals, and elements.

Picture energy as a subtle current that runs through reality, intangible yet tangible. It gives rise to seedlings, enlivens forests, and throbs within us all. The green witch acknowledges this universal energy and seeks alignment with its cycles, tuning into the ebb and flow of the natural world.

So why do we choose to practice natural magic? Because the energy found in nature carries a unique resonance—an age-old wisdom that speaks to our souls. When we access this storehouse of natural magic, we awaken to a deeper connection with the earth and its inhabitants. We become channels for the energy running through us, allowing us to seamlessly manifest our intentions in harmony with the planet.

By working with natural magic, we learn to respect and appreciate the earth. We witness how the seasons change, how the moon waxes and wanes, and how different creatures interact with each other in their ecosystems. We acknowledge the wisdom of plants, animals, and the land, recognizing that everything is connected. This connection to nature reminds us of our place in the world, as a part of an interconnected web of life.

As you begin your journey as a green witch, remember that energy is everywhere. The natural world holds secrets that are waiting to be unlocked if you know where to look. Listen to the rustling of leaves, smell the fragrance of blooming flowers, and feel the soil beneath your feet. These are all ways to connect with the energy that surrounds us. Embrace this innate power you hold within you, for you are a part of this interwoven fabric of life.

## Why Green Witches Use Energy: Working With Energy

The green witch sees the world quite differently than most people do. Most people live their lives quite unconsciously, paying more attention to their phones, or their work, or else their minds are stuck regretting the past, or worrying about the future. Green witches do our their best to remain in the present moment, for it is within the present moment where natural magic resides. We understand the energy that exists in the natural world around us that we can use to power our intentions and our magic when we stay in the present moment.

You may never have thought about it before, but it is true, energy is always all around us, in various forms. That's why it's such a no-brainer to simply learn to work with it and learn to harness it effectively for your intentions and desires. This could be anything from working with the earth's naturally stabilizing properties, the power of fire to purify and transform, water's ability to cleanse, the moon's ability to attract, or a gentle breeze's ability to calm when it whispers across your skin.

It is through spells, rituals and sacred practices, that we engage in a beautiful waltz with the elements, welcoming their powers to permeate our intentions and desires.

By working with natural magic, we learn to respect and appreciate the earth. We witness how the seasons change, how the moon waxes and wanes, and how different creatures interact with each other in their ecosystems. We acknowledge the wisdom of plants, animals, and the land, recognizing that everything is connected. This connection to nature reminds us of our place in the world, as a part of an interconnected web of life.

As you begin your journey as a green witch, remember that energy is everywhere. The natural world holds secrets that are waiting to be unlocked if you know where to look.

Listen to the rustling of leaves, smell the fragrance of blooming flowers, and feel the soil beneath your feet. These are all ways to connect with the energy that surrounds us.

## Working With the Energies Around You

Green witches have two powerful and effective methods of infusing intentions and actions to change the energy around us, including meditation and rituals.

Meditation: We use meditation to still our minds, center ourselves, and become attuned to the subtleties within and around us. While in a tranquil and focused state, we can visualize our goals, form positive affirmations, and purpose our energy towards our desired outcomes. This deliberate and intentional focus, combined with the peace created through meditation, gives our thoughts and tasks direction, and magnifies the energy, propelling it forward.

Ritual: Rituals are ceremonial acts that provide a pathway between the spiritual and physical realms. They offer a systematic way to manage energy, while also bringing our wishes into reality. Rituals commonly incorporate symbolic objects such as candles, crystals, herbs, and symbols with their own energetic properties. By combining these components with our rituals, we create an intense experience that helps anchor our intentions and control the direction of energy. Whether setting up an altar or casting a spell, rituals allow us to actively connect with the energy nearby in a thoughtful manner, ultimately giving rise to what we desire.

Both meditation and ritual supply us with potent pathways for mastering the energy inside and outside of us. They equip us with tools to breathe life into our intentions with clarity and motivation, creating a conduit for energy to move through so our dreams may be realized. With dedication and an open heart, we can deepen our bond with nature's powers and unlock the transformative potential of energy within our lives.

**Meditation for Manifestation: Channeling Energy towards Intentions**

Find a calming and peaceful place where you can relax without any interruptions, it could be in your backyard, a room in your home, or even your favorite spot in nature. Settle into a position that is natural for you, letting your body drift off into ease. Take a few deep breaths with closed eyes, allowing the release of all strain or tension.

1. Grounding and Centering (2-3 minutes): Start by imagining roots growing from your feet, spreading far into the ground. Feel the connection between you and the earth, inviting balance and stability. With each breath in, picture yourself pulling in comforting energy from the earth, and with every exhale, let go of any concerns or undesirable energies. Take some time to center yourself and make a solid

foundation.

2. 2. Setting Your Intention (2-3 minutes): Now, bring up the desired intention or ambition you have in mind. It could be anything from healing to abundance, love, happiness, or personal growth. Visualize this aim as a bright and glowing sphere of energy radiating with potentiality. Keep this image in your thoughts and feel the emotions related to obtaining your wish—may it be joy, appreciation, or harmony.

3. Infusing Energy (5-7 minutes): With your aim still held in your consciousness, imagine a stream of golden or brilliant energy streaming down from above coming into your head at the crown. Allow this energy to fill up your whole presence slowly, lighting up every cell with its white light. As you keep breathing, allow this energy to course across your body towards the core and outwards. While continuing to breathe, envision this energy extending beyond your physical body creating

an attractive radiance of life around you. Inside this sparkling aura see your goal shining even brighter and more powerful due to the energy that's been channeled.

4. Release and Trust (2-3 minutes): As you end your meditation, take a few moments to express gratitude for the energy that has flowed through you and for the manifestation of your desires. Trust that the universe is working in alignment with your intentions and that the powerful energy you have cultivated will continue to support and guide you.

Gently bring your attention back to the present moment, wiggling your fingers and toes, and slowly opening your eyes when you feel ready. Take a few more deep breaths, acknowledging the energy you have cultivated and the power within you to manifest your desires.

Remember, this meditation is a starting point, and you can change it to suit your own preferences and needs. Regular practice will strengthen your connection to the energy of nature all around you and deepen your ability to manifest your intentions. Embrace this beautiful journey of green witchcraft, where the power of energy and intention combine to create transformative magic in your life.

# Chapter Four

# Setting Up Your Magical Space

Crafting your own altar is a beautiful, and meaningful practice. Doing so allows you to create a special area in your home that is custom-built for your personal spiritual journey. Not only is it a reminder of your journey, but it is an area where you can perform rituals, meditate, perform spell work, and affirm your intentions, goals, and desires for what you want in life. This brief chapter will teach you the basics of how to make a powerful altar of your own, that resonates with your energy and furthers your growth as a green witch.

Find a quiet and private area in your home that offers a sense of peace and calm, a place that allows you to focus on your practice. You may want to consider natural light, since it can add a beautiful energy to your altar. Whichever place you choose, you will want to make sure the area remains undisturbed, since this allows your altar to retain its sacredness.

Start by cleansing the area of any negative energy. You can do this by smudging the area with sage, through sound through a singing bowl, meditation music, or simply by visualizing your space being filled with positive vibrations. Get rid of any physical clutter in the space, since it will help to create a peaceful environment.

Next, gather any items that hold a deep spiritual importance to you, things you may find "sacred" to you, like crystals, candles, amulets, ritual oils, and symbols that resonate with your beliefs and intentions. Feel free to include any tools you use in your rituals, like a wand, chalice, or tarot cards, to enhance your practice and connection.

Then, you'll need an altar surface or foundation for your items. You may want to choose a solid surface like a table, shelf, desk, countertop, or even a dedicated altar cloth if you must, as the foundation for your altar. You may want to use natural materials like wood, glass, or stone to bring a grounding energy to your sacred altar space.

Some green witches try to incorporate the four elements (Earth, Air, Fire, Water) on their altars in some fashion, in order to create a harmonious balance, and you are welcomed to do the same if it feels right.

- Earth: Crystals, plants, or soil.

- Air: Feathers, incense, or a feather fan.

- Fire: Candles or symbols of flames.

- Water: A small bowl of water or seashells.

Set up your items in a way that holds a personal meaning to you, a way that reflects your spiritual journey, preferences and intentions. You can add symbols or artifacts that align with your beliefs, desires, and areas of focus, like healing, love, abundance, self-development or protection.

It's important to regularly cleanse and charge your altar items as they can collect negative energies over-time. Cleansing your items and charging them can look like using methods like using moonlight, sunlight, or energy cleansing techniques. Keep the surface and your altar items clean and dust-free so they can keep their vibrant, high energy.

Try to create a habit of connecting with your altar each day, or at least on a certain day(s) each week, through meditation, prayer, or setting intentions. You can light candles, burn incense, or perform small rituals to infuse your altar with your energy and intentions.

It's so important to allow your altar to evolve and grow as your spiritual journey progresses. This could look like incorporating new symbols, statues, crystals or items that reflect your current intentions and spiritual journey. Your personal altar will become a sacred sanctuary - a reflection of yourself. It's a place of inspiration, manifestation, and profound connection.

As you use your altar on a regular basis, and infuse it with your desires, intentions, wishes, and energy, you will find that your altar becomes a priceless tool for you, and a source of constant inspiration and spiritual growth. May your altar bless you in ways you can only imagine!

# Chapter Five

# Crystals in Green Witch Magic

Crystals have long been used as a powerful tool for healing, protection, and spiritual growth. In the realm of green witchcraft, crystals are of particularly great importance due to their natural origin. The vibrations of these stones from the earth resonate with the same energy that binds us to nature and her elements. As such, they can be used to amplify our desires and intentions when it comes to achieving our magical goals.

Each type of crystal holds its own unique frequency and possesses its own magical properties that can enhance your spell work. Knowing which crystals work best for specific spells or rituals is essential to make the most out of them. For instance, rose quartz is often associated with attracting love - you might use this crystal in a spell to attract romantic partners into your life. On the other hand, black tourmaline may be used to provide protection against negative thoughts or energies - you could incorporate this crystal into a protection spell.

When purchasing or finding crystals to use in magic rituals, you may wish to start with a small collection that includes a crystal that represents one of the main chakras in the body. In other words, your initial collection should resemble the rainbow - red, orange, yellow, green, blue, purple, pink, and then add a clear crystal and a black crystal. This is a good starter set, as at least one of these crystals can work in most spells. It's important to note that larger crystals tend to carry more energy.

## Charging Your Crystals

Using energy to charge your crystals is necessary to take full advantage of their power for your magical rituals and spellwork. Every crystal has its own particular properties and vibrations, and charging them lets you transfer focused intention into them. This makes them a wonderful asset for your green witchcraft practice.

Sunlight: The sun's inviting rays are a very strong source of power for crystals. Choose one sunny morning to place your crystals outside or near a window where they can enjoy the revitalizing sunlight. Picture the sun's energy flowing into each crystal, cleaning it and giving it new life with its vitality.

Moonlight: The moon's soft light brings a nurturing and purifying energy perfect for cleansing and charging crystals. On the night of the full moon, find a safe spot outside, or near a window, where you can set up your crystals so they can absorb the moonlight. Draw on
the moon's energy and aim to fill  your crystals with its power.

Earth Connection: The Earth gives off grounding energy, ideal for centering and recharging your crystals.

Bury your crystals in the soil for one day, allowing them to connect to the Earth's protective essence. After you unearth them, sense how their bond to the Earth is now imbuing them with renewed vigor.

Crystal Clusters: Larger crystal clusters, particularly clear quartz, have the power to cleanse and recharge other crystals. Place your crystals on top of a bigger cluster or surround them with smaller crystals to amplify their energies. The crystal cluster serves as an intermediary, increasing the vibrations and intentions of each crystal within its reach.

## Cleansing Your Crystals

As you work with crystals, make sure to cleanse them regularly. Doing this removes any attachment from previous uses so they are ready for new energy and intention-setting.

Some people will cleanse their crystals before each use, while others do so every week, once a month, etc. It will ultimately depend on how frequently you are using yours. One way you can cleanse your crystals is by running them through sage smoke. Another way is by using natural light (either lunar or solar) to allow your crystals to soak up the light for 10 - 11 hours. If doing this at night, bring your crystals inside before 12pm the next day; that way they can benefit from both moonlight and sunlight.

Planting your crystals in the dirt helps to cleanse them further, just be sure to gently rinse with water and pat them dry afterward.

Another way is to place brown rice in a bowl, bury your crystals in it, and allow it to sit for 24 hours. After this time you may remove your newly cleansed crystals. It is believed that you should throw the rice away afterwards, since it is said to have absorbed the negative energies from the stones.

Finally, when not in use you can either keep your crystals on your altar, or store your crystals in special pouches or boxes. This will ensure that they stay safe and secure until next time.

## Crystal Grids: Sacred Geometry to Strengthen Your Intentions

Creating crystal grids is a powerful way to strengthen your intentions and enhance the energy of your spells and rituals. By combining the unique properties of different crystals and arranging them in sacred geometric patterns, you create a potent energetic matrix to manifest your desires. Anytime you look at your crystal grid, or meditate near it, know that it is infusing your desires, wishes and intentions with its amazing energies, helping them appear in your life much faster.

## Making Your Crystal Grid

Focal Crystal: Begin by selecting a central crystal that resonates with your specific intention. This focal crystal will anchor the grid and set the tone for your magical working.

Supporting Crystals: Choose supporting crystals that complement and amplify the energies of the focal crystal. Consider their correspondences and intuitive connection with your intention.

Intuitive Design: While certain geometric patterns like a flower of life or a spiral can enhance the grid's energy, you can also intuitively create a design that feels right for your purpose. Follow your instincts and let your inner guidance lead the way.

Activation and Intent: Once the crystals are arranged, infuse the grid with your intention and visualize the energy flowing between the crystals. Connect with each crystal's essence and set your intention for the manifestation of your desires.

## Crystal Scrying For Insight and Visions

Crystal scrying is a powerful practice that allows us to access the higher realms of consciousness and gain powerful insights. If you hold a smooth crystal like quartz or amethyst in your hands, you can open up spiritual gateways within yourself and discover deep wisdom from within.

Prior to your scrying session, you may wish to use your *Visions Oil*, or your *Dreamtime Tea* in order to take advantage of their divination properties and truly make the most of it.

Picking Your Crystal: For scrying, pick a smooth, clear crystal - the more transparent it is, the better. Quartz and amethyst are particularly popular choices for this activity due to their clarity and purity.

Creating Sacred Space: To achieve maximum benefit from your scrying experience, create a serene and sacred space for yourself. Dim the lights, light some candles and fill the area with items that bring out feelings of tranquility.

Activating Meditation Mode: Make sure you're sitting comfortably then gently hold the crystal in your hands. Take some deep breaths then let your mind grow quiet, and your eyes gently focus on the crystal surface.

Gathering Intuitive Vision: As you gaze into the crystal, trust the images, symbols or messages that come to you - these could be valuable guidance and answers to your questions. Allow your intuition to take over as you interpret these visions.

Tip: Much like having a dream book, you may choose to dedicate a journal to your scrying practices. After every session, make some notes, writing down anything you experienced during your experience. Revisit these pages on periodically, noting how many visions came to pass in your life (if you received visions) and/or reflecting on how much insight your sessions have added to your growth as a green witch and a being who is connected to both the world around you and the higher realms.

## Crystals Every Green Witch Needs

**Amber:** Assists in manifesting, mood-boosting, attracts romantic love, amplifies beauty, strengthens psychic abilities, banishes negative energy, inspires wisdom and calmness, inspires creativity

**Amethyst:** Associated with spiritual growth, promotes calmness, protection, intuition, and dreams. Often used in green witchcraft to enhance meditation and helps with restful sleep.

**Aventurine:** Associated with luck, abundance, attracts opportunities, prosperity, and positive outcomes. Promotes emotional healing, inner peace, and optimism.

**Black Onyx:** Grounding, protection, shields against negativity, and fosters self-discipline. Brings strength, stability, and protection during hard times.

**Black Tourmaline:** Associated with protection, grounding, shields against negative energies, psychic attacks, and electromagnetic radiation. It promotes energetic balance and purification.

**Carnelian:** Associated with motivation, creativity, empowerment and vitality. Sparks passion, confidence, and helps you to overcome obstacles.

**Celestite:** Associated with being connected to the Universe/Source/Nature, and higher consciousness, enhances spiritual communication, intuition, and inner peace.

Encourages angelic guidance, aids you in astral travel.

**Citrine:** Associated with abundance, and wealth, manifestation, joy, prosperity, success, and bringing positive energy into your life.

**Clear Quartz:** Often called the "Master Healer" crystal, known to amplify energy, promotes clarity, and deepen spiritual connections.

**Fluorite:** Protective, stabilizing, promotes mental clarity, focus, and psychic development. Aids in decision-making, organization, and energetic cleansing.

**Hematite:** Creates harmony in the mind, body, and spirit, grounding, aids in manifestation, strength, and protects against negativity.

**Labradorite:** Associated with divination, enhancing intuition, spiritual growth, and psychic abilities. Helps to uncover your potential and aids you in embracing change.

**Lapis Lazuli:** Associated with wisdom, truth, and spiritual enlightenment. Enhances intuition, psychic abilities, and supports profound inner transformation.

**Malachite:** Associated with transformation, healing, and protection with this dynamic crystal. Encourages emotional healing, releases past traumas, and promotes positive transformation.

**Moonstone:** Associated with the divine feminine energy, intuition, balances, emotions. Enhances fertility, inner harmony, and harnesses the cycles of the moon.

**Pyrite:** Known as "Fool's Gold," a powerful stone that attracts wealth, abundance, and prosperity. It boosts confidence, and manifestation abilities.

**Rhodonite:** Associated with emotional healing and releasing emotional wounds, compassion, promotes forgiveness, self-love, personal growth and understanding.

**Rose Quartz:** Associated with love, promotes compassion and self-love, healing. Attracts positive relationships, cultivates a sense of peace and tenderness.

**Selenite:** Known to purify, protect, offers clarity, spiritual connection, and energy purification. Use it to cleanse other crystals and spaces with ease.

**Smoky Quartz:** Associated with grounding, banishes negative energy, fights electromagnetic pollution, helps get rid of old patterns and habits, promotes emotional health.

**Note:** Not all crystals should be owned, or handled due to their toxic properties which can be toxic to humans. This is all the more reason why you should exercise caution, do your research, and be aware of potential hazards when working with and owning certain crystals, especially the rarer ones that are harder to obtain. If you are unsure about a crystal and its effects on human health, please consult a knowledgeable professional like a mineralogist. Also, be careful about ingesting crystals in elixirs unless you are sure it is safe to do so.

### Crystals With Toxic Properties

**Malachite**: Malachite contains copper, which can be toxic if ingested or handled without caution. It is best to have it in its tumbled or polished form, rather than raw pieces, and always wash your hands after handling.

**Cinnabar**: Cinnabar contains mercury, which is highly toxic. It should never be used in its raw form or ingested. Cinnabar should only be handled with gloves and kept out of reach of children.

**Galena**: Galena contains lead, and should not be handled frequently. Avoid touching it with your bare hands, or wash your hands thoroughly after handling it.

**Selenite**: Selenite is a soft mineral that can easily break into sharp pieces, causing splinters. Handle selenite with care to avoid injury.

**Pyrite**: Pyrite is a wonderful wealth-drawing crystal, but it can release harmful fumes when heated. So avoid heating or burning pyrite.

**Crocidolite (Blue Asbestos)**: Crocidolite is a fibrous mineral that is considered highly dangerous and toxic. It should *never* be handled or used in any form.

# Chapter Six

# Magical Herbs and Their Unique Properties

Herbs have so many purposes. Most regular people overlook herbs, or else they only see them as plants growing in the ground, or small greens used to garnish and flavor food. This is unfortunate because it only speaks to how removed most people in our society are from nature, that they can overlook herbs each day, completely unaware of the myriad of benefits these herbs possess. Meanwhile, herbs have always held a sacred place in the practices of green witches. We understand that herbs possess so many amazing, magical, and practical uses. This is why, throughout the ages, herbs have been revered for their potent properties, like enhancing our spellwork, healing ailments, and their profound ability to connect us with the natural world.

In this chapter, we will delve into a wide array of magical herbs, and explore their significance in the craft of green witches and the transformative power they possess. You will uncover their unique identifiers, any possible healing properties, and their spiritual or magical qualities in regard to rituals and spellwork. From fragrant blooms to potent roots, from vibrant leaves to mysterious barks, each herb carries a unique vibration and energy that aligns with specific intentions and purposes.

As green witches, we recognize the interconnectedness of all living beings and the deep wisdom that emanates from the earth. We understand the inherent power of plants and their ability to heal, nourish, and guide us on our spiritual path. Through our interactions with these botanical allies, we forge a profound relationship with the natural world, tapping into the ancient knowledge that has been passed down through generations.

But herbal magic is more than just the physical properties of the herbs themselves. It is an intimate relationship with the natural world, a dance of energy and intention, where the lines between the mundane and the magical blur. It is an invitation to reconnect with the earth, to honor its gifts, and to harness its wisdom in our craft.

Hopefully, by the end of this chapter, you will see and experience the herbs in your life much differently. Seeing them for all they are and all they do for us. After better understanding herbs, allow each one you use in your daily life to become a guide, leading you closer to the heart of your craft, and opening doors to realms of healing, divination, and spiritual growth.

**Acacia**

Properties: Protection, psychic enhancement, purification.

Medicinal Uses: Used in traditional medicine for respiratory issues and wound healing.

Magical Uses: Enhances psychic abilities, purification rituals, and spiritual protection.

Identification: Acacia is a tree and shrub with clusters of small, fragrant flowers.

Harvesting: Collect the bark or flowers as needed once the plant reaches maturity. Please note that this can take years.

Where to Find: Acacia trees are native to Africa, but various species can be found worldwide. Acacia products can be purchased from herbal or spiritual supply stores, and it is much easier to obtain them this way as well.

**Acorn**

Properties: Prosperity, fertility, grounding.

Medicinal Uses: antibacterial, anti-viral, believed to help improve digestion.

Magical Uses: Luck, abundance, attracts positive energy.

Identification: Acorns are the nuts of oak trees.

Harvesting: You can easily collect acorns in Autumn after they fall from the trees.

Where to Find: Typically beneath oak trees in forests or parks.

**Agar Agar**

Properties: Gelatinous, soothing, and nutrient-rich.

Medicinal Uses: Supports digestion and can be used as a vegan alternative to gelatin.

Magical Uses: Binding spells, joy, success, protection, and stability.

Identification: A gelatinous substance that comes from seaweed.

Harvesting: Produced and available commercially in a powdered or flake form.

Where to Find: Can be purchased from health food stores or online.

## Agrimony

Properties: Protective, healing, and promoting emotional well-being.

Medicinal Uses: Relieves digestive issues, supports liver health, and aids sleep.

Magical Uses: Protection, banishes negativity, and enhances psychic abilities.

Identification: Agrimony is a perennial herb with clusters of small, yellow flowers and serrated leaves.

Harvesting: Gather the aerial parts (leaves and flowers) when the plant is in full bloom. Where to Find: Agrimony can be found growing in fields, meadows, or herb gardens, or purchased from herbal stores.

## Allspice

Properties: Warming, digestive, and stimulating.

Medicinal Uses: Supports digestion, heart health, dental health. Increases circulation, anti-inflammatory and antioxidant

Magical Uses: Abundance, attracts good fortune, and boosts energy.

Identification: Allspice is a spice derived from dried berries of the Pimenta dioica tree, resembling a blend of cloves, cinnamon, and nutmeg.

Harvesting: Allspice berries are commercially available as dried spice. Where to Find: Allspice can be purchased from grocery stores or spice suppliers.

## Anchusa Azurea

Properties: Uplifting, stimulating, and attracts joy.

Medicinal Uses: Not commonly used medicinally.

Magical Uses: Enhancing mood, attracting positivity, and promoting happiness.

Identification: Anchusa Azurea is a herbaceous perennial plant with clusters of bright blue flowers.

Harvesting: Anchusa Azurea is mostly grown for display purposes.

Where to Find: Native to Europe, it can be found on roadsides, hills, etc.

## Anise (Aniseed)

Properties: Uplifting, stimulating, and attracts joy.

Medicinal Uses: decreases bloating and other digestive issues, antiseptic and helps to treat coughs, stimulates the appetite, eases menstrual pain, aphrodisiac, insomnia and more!

Magical Uses: Increases psychic abilities, wards off negativity and the evil eye, and promotes prophetic visions.

Identification: Anise are from the Apiaceae family, a flowering plant.

Harvesting: Harvest the seeds when they have turned brown and are easy to extract. This is usually around late summer or early fall, after the heads have flowered.

Where to Find: Native to Egypt, Asia and the Mediterranean, but can be bought at herbal stores or special suppliers.

## Arrowroot

Properties: Soothing, nutritious, and easily digestible.

Medicinal Uses: Aids digestion, supports hydration, and can be used as a thickening agent.

Magical Uses: Clarity, purification, and protection.

Identification: Arrowroot is a starch obtained from the rhizomes of various tropical plants.

Harvesting: Arrowroot powder is commercially available.

Where to Find: Arrowroot powder can be bought at grocery stores and most health food stores.

## Balm of Gilead Tears

Properties: Healing, soothing, and comforting.

Medicinal Uses: Traditionally used for skin healing, inflammation, and respiratory issues.

Magical Uses: love spells and rituals, grief healing, emotional healing, relaxation, and spiritual comfort.

Identification: A resinous substance obtained from the buds of the balsam poplar or related species.

Harvesting: Can be purchased from herbal suppliers.

Where to Find: Can be found through certain specialized herbal suppliers.

## Barley

Properties: Nourishing, grounding, and soothing.

Medicinal Uses: Supports digestion, provides energy, and promotes healthy skin.

Magical Uses: Fertility, abundance, and prosperity.

Identification: Barley is a cereal grain with small, oval-shaped seeds.

Harvesting: Commercially produced and available as whole grains or flour.

Where to Find: Can be purchased from grocery stores or health food stores.

## Bayberry

Properties: Cleansing, protection, and abundance.

Medicinal Uses: Used for sore throat and gastrointestinal issues for years.

Magical Uses: Money spells, attracting good fortune, and spiritual purification.

Identification: Bayberry is a shrub with aromatic leaves and waxy gray berries.

Harvesting: Collect the berries when they have ripened.

Where to Find: Bayberry products, such as candles or wax, can be purchased from specialty suppliers.

## Bay Leaves

Properties: Protection, purification, and enhancing psychic abilities.

Medicinal Uses: Supports digestion, aids respiratory health, and has antimicrobial properties.

Magical Uses: Attracts wealth and abundance, enhances spells, divination, increases psychic abilities, and wards off negative energies.

Identification: Bay leaves are dried leaves from the bay laurel tree.

Harvesting: Bay leaves are commercially available as dried spice.

Where to Find: Bay leaves can be purchased from grocery stores or spice suppliers.

## Bergamot

Properties: Uplifting, aromatic, and calming.

Medicinal Uses: Relieves anxiety, soothes digestion, and eases headaches.

Magical Uses: Protection, relaxation, and attracting positive energy.

Identification: Bergamot is a perennial herb with feathery leaves and clusters of brightly colored flowers.

Harvesting: Gather the aerial parts (leaves and flowers) when the plant is in full bloom.

Where to Find: It can be found growing in gardens, or you can buy it from herbal stores.

## Black Cohosh

Properties: Possesses a deep connection to the realms of healing, protection, and feminine energy.

Medicinal Uses: Alleviates symptoms associated with menopause like hot flashes, mood swings, sleep disturbances, has anti-inflammatory properties, aids menstrual issues.

Magical Uses: Feminine power, fertility, and protection. Used in rituals, and spells invoke or honor the divine feminine, enhancing intuition and connecting with ancestral wisdom.

Identification: Scientifically called Actaea racemosa, is a tall, perennial plant with white flower clusters that grows in woodland areas.

Harvesting: The roots should be harvested in the fall after the flowering period.

Where to Find: Native to North America, in woodland areas with moist soil, and at local herb shops or apothecaries.

## Black Pepper

Properties: Warming, stimulating, and digestive.

Medicinal Uses: Aids digestion, boosts metabolism, and relieves congestion.

Magical Uses: Excellent for banishing negativity, protection, and enhancing spell work.

Identification: Black pepper is a spice derived from dried berries of the Piper nigrum vine.

Harvesting: Black pepper is commercially available as dried spice.

Where to Find: Black pepper can be purchased from grocery stores or spice suppliers.

## Bladderwrack

Properties: A seaweed rich in minerals and nutrient

Medicinal Uses: Traditionally used as a medicine. A natural source of iodine which is important for thyroid function, and rich in nutrients that increases overall health. Boosts metabolism.

Magical Uses: Purifying and protective. Wards off negative energies, promotes spiritual cleansing, and enhances vitality. Offers energetic protection, enhances intuition, and encourages overall well-being.

Identification: A brown seaweed commonly found in the rocky regions, on the coast of the Atlantic and Pacific oceans, has distinctive air-filled bladders or "bubbles" along its fronds, which help it float in water.

Harvesting: Best to collect bladderwrack that has washed ashore, instead of trying to harvest it directly from the ocean. Carefully select healthy and intact portions of the seaweed, avoiding any contaminated or damaged pieces.

Where to Find: Found in specialty health food stores, herbal shops, or online stores that offer seaweed products in its dried form, powdered form, capsules, etc.

Safety: Excessive consumption may result in iodine imbalances.

## Burdock Root

Properties: Detoxifying, nutritive, and skin-healing.

Medicinal Uses: Supports liver health, aids in skin conditions, and promotes healthy hair.

Magical Uses: Protection, warding off negativity, and banishing.

Identification: A biennial plant with large leaves and prickly burrs.

Harvesting: Roots should ideally be collected within the first year or at least in early spring of the second year.

Where to Find: Burdock can be found growing wild in fields or easily purchased from herbal stores.

## Calamus Root

Properties: Stimulating, uplifting, and promoting mental clarity.

Medicinal Uses: Supports digestion, aids mental focus, and relieves stress.

Magical Uses: Enhances concentration, promotes clarity in communication, and attracts good luck.

Identification: A perennial herb with tall, sword-like leaves and aromatic rhizomes. Harvesting: Gather the rhizomes in late Autumn or early spring.

Where to Find: Calamus Root can be found growing in wetlands or purchased from herbal stores.

## Calendula

Properties: detoxifying, inspiring.

Medicinal Uses: skin detoxifying, anti-inflammatory, menstrual relief, antibacterial, moves the lymphatic system, wound healing

Magical Uses: Creativity, promotes joy, prophetic dreams, enhances confidence and beauty, increases leadership qualities, household protection

Identification: A bright, yellowy-orange flower from the daisy family, also called a Marigold

Harvesting: Gather the flowers when they are in full bloom

Where to Find: Native to North and South America and can be purchased from herbal stores

## Catnip

Properties: Calming, relaxing, and promoting sleep.

Medicinal Uses: Relieves anxiety, aids sleep, and soothes digestive issues.

Magical Uses: Enhances cat magic, attracts love and luck, and promotes relaxation.

Identification: A perennial herb with aromatic, heart-shaped leaves.

Harvesting: Gather the leaves and flowers after they bloom, but before they wilt.

Where to Find: Catnip can be grown in gardens or purchased as dried leaves or herbal tea.

## Cat's Claw

Properties: Immune-boosting, anti-inflammatory, and adaptogenic.

Medicinal Uses: Supports immune health, relieves inflammation, and promotes vitality.

Magical Uses: Protection, wards off negative energies, and enhances intuition.

Identification: A woody vine with curved thorns resembling a cat's claw.

Harvesting: Cat's Claw supplements are available commercially.

Where to Find: Supplements can be purchased from health food stores.

## Cayenne

Properties: Stimulating, warming, and pain-relieving.

Medicinal Uses: Supports circulation, aids digestion, and has topical analgesic properties.

Magical Uses: Protection, banishes negativity, and enhances spells.

Identification: A spice derived from ground-dried chili peppers.

Harvesting: Cayenne powder is commercially available as a dried spice.

Where to Find: Cayenne powder can be purchased from grocery stores or spice suppliers.

## Chamomile

Properties: Calming, soothing, and promotes relaxation.

Medicinal Uses: Relieves anxiety, aids sleep, and soothes digestive issues.

Magical Uses: Promotes peace, relaxation, promotes good luck and enhances dream work.

Identification: Chamomile is a flowering plant with small, daisy-like flowers.

Harvesting: Gather the flowers when they are in full bloom.

Where to Find: Can be grown in herb gardens or purchased as dried flowers or herbal tea.

## Cinnamon

Properties: Warming, stimulating, and energizing.

Medicinal Uses: Supports digestion, aids circulation, and has antimicrobial properties.

Magical Uses: Attracts abundance, wealth, love, enhances spellwork, and promotes success.

Identification: Cinnamon is a spice derived from the bark of cinnamon trees.

Harvesting: Cinnamon sticks or powder are commercially available.

Where to Find: Sticks or powder can be purchased from grocery stores or spice suppliers.

Safety: Cinnamon may interfere with some diabetes medications.

## Clove

Properties: Warming, stimulating, and analgesic.

Medicinal Uses: Relieves toothaches, supports digestion, and has antimicrobial properties.

Magical Uses: Protection, enhances psychic abilities, and attracts wealth.

Identification: Clove is an aromatic spice derived from dried flower buds belonging to the Syzygium aromaticum tree.

Harvesting: Commercially available as dried spice.

Where to Find: Can be purchased from grocery stores or spice suppliers.

## Coffee

Properties: Energizing, stimulating, and comforting. It is associated with invigoration, focus, and social connection.

Medicinal Uses: Aids in alertness, focus and mental clarity, invigorating. It contains the natural stimulant caffeine, that can boost your energy levels, improve cognitive function, and enhance mood.

Magical Uses: Increases energy, focus, and manifestation power. Awakens the senses, stimulates creativity, and aids in divination. Can bring clarity to intentions in rituals, promote productivity, and connect with the energies of inspiration and manifestation.

Identification: Coffee comes from the seeds of coffee plants.

Harvesting: No need to harvest your own typically, as they are readily available.

Where to Find: Coffee beans and ground coffee can be found in grocery stores, specialty coffee shops, and online retailers.

Safety: Should be consumed in moderation. Effects may vary among individuals ex. too much can cause digestive upset in some people.

## Damiana

Properties: Aphrodisiac, mood-enhancing, and promoting relaxation.

Medicinal Uses: Supports reproductive health, aids mood balance, and has mild diuretic properties.

Magical Uses: Enhances love spells, promotes passion, and invokes relaxation.

Identification: Damiana is a small shrub with aromatic leaves and yellow flowers.

Harvesting: Gather the aerial parts (leaves and flowers) when the plant is in full bloom.

Where to Find: Damiana can be found growing in warm climates or purchased as dried leaves or herbal supplements.

## Dandelion

Properties: Detoxifying, diuretic, and nutritive.

Medicinal Uses: Supports liver health, aids digestion, and promotes detoxification.

Magical Uses: Depends which part of the plant is used but in general: divination, spirit connection, dreamwork, creativity, psychic abilities, wishes, courage

Identification: An herbaceous plant with jagged leaves and yellow flowers that turn into fluffy seed heads.

Harvesting: Gather the leaves before flowering and the roots in Fall.

Where to Find: Grows abundantly in lawns, meadows, and fields.

## Deer's Tongue Leaf

Properties: Enhancing communication, psychic awareness, and attracting love.

Medicinal Uses: Historically used as an expectorant and for mouth and throat conditions.

Magical Uses: Enhances divination, attracts love and passion, and promotes eloquence.

Identification: Deer's Tongue is a perennial herb with elongated leaves resembling a deer's tongue.

Harvesting: Can be purchased from herbal stores or online.

Where to Find: Can be purchased in specialty herbal stores.

## Dogtooth Violet

Properties: Renewal, protection, and connecting with the earth.

Medicinal Uses: Not commonly used medicinally.

Magical Uses: Enhancing spells for renewal, protection, and grounding.

Identification: Dogtooth Violet is a perennial plant with mottled leaves and yellow or white flowers resembling a dog's tooth.

Harvesting: Dogtooth Violet is primarily grown as an ornamental plant.

Where to Find: Dogtooth Violet can be found in gardens or nurseries specializing in ornamental plants.

## Dragon's Blood Tree

Properties: Protection, strength, and empowerment.

Medicinal Uses: Antidiarrhetic, anti-inflammatory, antimicrobial, heals wounds, antioxidant

Magical Uses: Spell work, rituals for courage and power, banishes negative energies.

Identification: Dragon's Blood Tree is an evergreen tree with a distinctive umbrella-shaped crown and red resin.

Harvesting: Obtain dragon's blood resin from trusted herbal suppliers.

Where to Find: Dragon's Blood Tree is native to Socotra Island and can be found through specialized herbal suppliers.

**Datura**

Properties: Hallucinogenic, toxic, and associated with visionary experiences.

Medicinal Uses: Not recommended for medicinal use due to its toxicity.

Magical Uses: Astral travel, spirit communication, and divination.

Identification: Datura is a group of flowering plants with trumpet-shaped flowers and spiky seed pods.

Harvesting: Exercise extreme caution and avoid harvesting or using datura due to its extreme toxicity.

Where to Find: Datura is not recommended for casual use due to its extreme toxicity.

## Deadly Nightshade or Belladonna

Properties: Poisonous, protective, and associated with witchcraft.

Medicinal Uses: Historically used for pain relief.

Magical Uses: Astral travel, spirit work, and invoking transformation.

Identification: Deadly Nightshade is a perennial herb with bell-shaped purple or greenish flowers and shiny black berries.

Harvesting: Exercise extreme caution and consult experts. It is highly toxic.

Where to Find: Found in woodland areas of Europe, the Middle East and North Africa. Not recommended for casual use due to its toxicity.

## Evening Primrose

Properties: Nourishing, soothing, and promoting hormonal balance.

Medicinal Uses: Supports hormonal health, relieves PMS symptoms, and helps with skin issues.

Magical Uses: Enhances beauty, promotes love and romance, and connects with lunar energy.

Identification: Evening Primrose is a biennial or perennial herb with bright yellow flowers that bloom in the evening.

Harvesting: Gather the flowers when they are fully open and the seeds after they have matured.

Where to Find: Evening Primrose can be found growing in fields and meadows, herb gardens, or purchased from herbal stores.

**Figwort**

Properties: Protective, grounding, and promoting emotional well-being.

Medicinal Uses: Supports lymphatic health, aids skin conditions, and relieves inflammation.

Magical Uses: Banishes negative energies, promotes healing, and enhances meditation.

Identification: Figwort is a perennial herb with clusters of tubular flowers and dark green leaves.

Harvesting: Gather the aerial parts (leaves and flowers) during the blooming season.

Where to Find: Can be found growing wild in fields or purchased from herbal stores.

## Geranium

Properties: Balancing, soothing, and uplifting.

Medicinal Uses: Used for its therapeutic benefits. Antibacterial and anti-inflammatory. Heals skin issues and wounds. Calms the nervous system, relieves stress and anxiety.

Magical Uses: Attracts love, increases fertility, and emotionally healing and balancing. Enhances self-love, promotes harmony, enhances positive energy, creates a loving and nurturing environment.

Identification: Vibrant flowers of various species and colors (white, red, pink, purple, etc.) in the Pelargonium genus family.

Harvesting: Harvest healthy leaves once the plant is in full bloom by gently from the stem.

Where to Find: Products from geranium can be found in gardens, herbal shops, and online retailers.

## Ginkgo Biloba

Properties: Ginkgo biloba properties anti-inflammatory, antioxidant, brain function.

Medicinal Uses: Supports memory, mental alertness, concentration., eye health. Believed to aid in circulation and support cardiovascular health.

Magical Uses: Associated with wisdom, longevity, and adaptability. Enhances mental agility, promotes open-mindedness, and encourages one to embrace change.

Identification: Tall trees that have distinct fan-shaped leaves that turn golden yellow in the fall. The trees are covered in a fleshy seeds that have an unpleasant odor when crushed.

Harvesting: Leaves are typically collected from mature trees during Autumn once they turn vibrant gold. in color.

Where to Find: Can be found in parks, gardens, and urban landscapes. Or in health stores as supplements, herbs and extracts.

Safety Information: Generally safe when used in appropriate doses for short periods. But might interact with certain medicines like blood thinners, and anti-seizure drugs. If you have a bleeding disorder, or you are scheduled for surgery should consult a doctor about taking ginkgo biloba. Do not consume raw seeds as they are poisonous.

**Ginger**

Properties: Warming, anti-inflammatory, and digestive.

Medicinal Uses: Relieves nausea, aids digestion, and reduces inflammation.

Magical Uses: Protection, love spells, and enhances magical energy, increases the speed of magic's results.

Identification: Ginger is the root of the Zingiber officinale plant with a spicy, strong taste that makes it popular in cooking.

Harvesting: Ginger roots are commercially available fresh, powdered or dried.

Where to Find: Can be purchased from grocery stores or herbal suppliers.

Safety: Consult a healthcare professional before using if pregnant or breastfeeding. Avoid excessive consumption if you have a bleeding disorder.

**Gotu Kola**

Properties: Soothing and rejuvenating, and known as the "Herb of Longevity."

Medicinal Uses: Skin-nourishing so it supports skin health and is used in skincare to aid in wound-healing, prevent scarring, psoriasis and stretch marks, promotes healthy brain function as you age, promotes healthy circulation, and aids in reducing inflammation. Studies have shown it may treat organ diseases of the liver, bladder etc. but more research is needed.

Magical Uses: Associated with healing and vitality. Often used in rituals and spells to promote emotional balance, boosts self-confidence, and attracts positive energies.

Identification: Features small, kidney-shaped leaves that grow close to the ground in clusters. It produces delicate pinkish or white flowers.

Harvesting: Carefully pluck the leaves from the plant,

making sure not to harm the root system.

Where to Find: Can be found in herb gardens, natural food stores, and herbal apothecaries. It is also available in the form of teas, tinctures, and as skincare products.

## Hawthorne

Properties: Heart-healthy, protective, balances high blood pressure and promotes emotional well-being.

Medicinal Uses: Supports cardiovascular health, aids digestion, and reduces anxiety.

Magical Uses: Protection, love spells, and helps you connect with the faerie realm.

Identification: Hawthorne is a shrub or small tree with thorny branches and clusters of white or pink flowers.

Harvesting: Gather the berries in late summer or early Autumn.

Where to Find: Hawthorne berries can be purchased from herbal stores or specialty suppliers.

Safety: Consult a healthcare professional before using medicinally, especially if pregnant or breastfeeding. Avoid use with certain heart medications.

## Henbane

Properties: Hallucinogenic, toxic, and associated with trance-like states.

Medicinal Uses: Not recommended for medicinal use due to its toxicity.

Magical Uses: Divination, spirit communication (extreme caution required).

Identification: Henbane is a biennial or perennial herb with bell-shaped flowers and large, lobed leaves.

Harvesting: Exercise extreme caution and avoid harvesting or using henbane due to its extreme toxicity.

Where to Find: Henbane can be found in specialty stores and through certain herbal suppliers.

## Hemlock

Properties: Poisonous, banishing, and purifying.

Medicinal Uses: Not recommended for medicinal use due to its extreme toxicity.

Magical Uses: Banishes negative energies, breaks hexes, and dispels evil.

Identification: Hemlock is a biennial or perennial plant with fern-like leaves and small white flowers.

Harvesting: Exercise extreme caution and avoid harvesting hemlock.

Where to Find: Hemlock can be found in specialty stores and through certain herbal suppliers.

## Hibiscus

Properties: Cooling, refreshing, and heart-healthy.

Medicinal Uses: Supports cardiovascular health, aids digestion, and promotes hydration.

Magical Uses: Love spells, divination, and attracting positive energy.

Identification: Hibiscus is a flowering plant with large, showy blossoms in various colors.

Harvesting: Gather the flowers when they are fully open.

Where to Find: Can be grown in gardens or purchased as dried flowers or herbal tea.

Safety: Consult a healthcare professional before using medicinally, especially if pregnant or breastfeeding.

## High John All Purpose Herb

Properties: Luck, success, and protection.

Medicinal Uses: Used to reduce pain and inflammation, anti-viral, antidepressant, boosts energy, reduces stress and anxiety.

Magical Uses: Loved by rootworkers, and widely used in Hoodoo magic, it is known to increase confidence, health, money, gambling, luck, protection and strength. As the name goes, it is great for everything.

Identification: Classified as an Ipomoea, a flowering plant that contains more than 600 species.

Harvesting: Obtain High John All Purpose Herb from trusted spiritual supply stores or herbal suppliers.

Where to Find: Can be found through specialized spiritual suppliers.

Safety: High John All Purpose Herb is primarily used in magical practices and not for medicinal purposes.

## Hydrangea

Properties: Harmonizing, soothing, and promoting emotional well-being.

Medicinal Uses: Historically used as a diuretic and for urinary tract health, lowers blood sugar levels, and antioxidant properties.

Magical Uses: Excellent for breaking curses and hexes, ending Karmic cycles, promotes emotional healing, balances energy, and enhances love spells.

Identification: Hydrangea is a shrub with large clusters of flowers in various colors.

Harvesting: Hydrangea supplements, dried or extracts are available commercially.

Where to Find: Hydrangea in various forms can be purchased from herbal stores or online.

Safety: Consult a healthcare professional before using medicine, especially if pregnant or breastfeeding.

## Iris Root

Properties: Enhancing intuition, promoting communication, and connecting with the divine feminine.

Medicinal Uses: Skin issues, digestive issues, headaches

Magical Uses: Divination, psychic development, and invoking the energy of the moon.

Identification: Iris is a genus of flowering plants with distinctive, colorful blooms.

Harvesting: Roots and rhizomes can be purchased from herbal stores or online.

Where to Find: Can be found through specialized herbal suppliers.

## Jasmine

Properties: Stress-relieving, relaxing, enchanting and love-drawing.

Medicinal Uses: Used for its soothing properties, promotes relaxation, alleviates stress. Believed to have mild sedative effects, aids promote good sleep and calms nerves.

Magical Uses: Associated with love and sensuality, attracts positive energies. Enhances romantic relationships, promotes self-love and confidence, and invites feelings of joy and happiness. Money-drawing, used in moon magic, promotes deep meditative states and prophetic dreams.

Identification: A vine or shrub with dark green leaves and clusters of fragrant, small, white flowers that bloom predominantly at night.

Harvesting: Can be gently picked by hand during their blooming season, usually in the evening or early morning when their scent is strongest.

Where to Find: Found in nature in warmer climates. Also can be purchased in stores as an oil or herb.

## Jezebel Root

Properties: Attracting love, enhancing sexuality, and promoting passion.

Medicinal Uses: Not commonly used medicinally.

Magical Uses: Love spells, seduction, and empowering feminine energy.

Identification: Jezebel Root is not a specific botanical term, but may refer to various roots associated with love and sexuality in magical practices.

Harvesting: Can be bought from trusted spiritual supply stores or herbal suppliers.

Where to Find: Specialized spiritual suppliers.

## Kava Kava

Properties: Relaxing, sedative, and euphoric.

Medicinal Uses: Promotes relaxation, alleviates anxiety, and induces sleep. Inspires calmness, stress relief, and social connections. Believed to have muscle-relaxing and mild analgesic effects.

Magical Uses: Induces tranquility, facilitates meditation, and enhances spiritual experiences. Promotes emotional healing, reduces stress, and creates a peaceful environment.

Identification: A plant, scientifically known as Piper methysticum, with heart-shaped leaves that produces small clusters of flowers.

Harvesting: Dig up the plant's root, dry and ground it, then process it into a powder or liquid to consume.

Where to Find: Found in Fiji, Vanuatu, and Tonga. It is also available as capsules, extracts, or teas in reputable health food stores, herbal shops, and online retailers.

## Job's Tears

Properties: Healing, protective, and bringing good fortune.

Medicinal Uses: Not commonly used medicinally.

Magical Uses: Protection, wards off evil and negative energies, and promotes abundance.

Identification: Job's Tears is a grass-like plant with hard, bead-like seeds.

Harvesting: Job's Tears seeds can be purchased from herbal suppliers or specialty stores.

Where to Find: Job's Tears seeds can be found through specialized herbal suppliers.

## Juniper

Properties: Purifying, protective, and enhancing spirituality.

Medicinal Uses: Supports urinary tract health, aids digestion, and has antimicrobial properties.

Magical Uses: Protection, relaxation, cleansing, and attracts positive energy and raises your vibration.

Identification: Juniper is a coniferous shrub or tree with small, bluish berries.

Harvesting: Collect the berries when they are ripe.

Where to Find: Can be purchased from herbal stores or specialty spice suppliers.

Safety: Consult a healthcare professional before using medicinally, especially if pregnant or breastfeeding.

## Lavender

Properties: antibacterial, and antifungal.

Medicinal Uses: Relieves pain from burns, calming effects and relaxes the muscles, aroma destresses, anti-inflammatory, helps relieve dandruff.

Magical Uses: Promotes a meditative state, enhances love and sex spells, inspires peace, friendship, used for insight, fertility, protects against negative behavior from loved ones, healing and during Summer solstice rituals.

Identification: Deep purple, sweet aromatic flowers from the Lamiaceae family.

Harvesting: Cut the flowers close to the base once it fully matures.

Where to Find: Can be grown in gardens or purchased as dried leaves or essential oil. Usually found in the Africa, Europe, and Asia.

## Lemongrass

Properties: Uplifting, antibacterial, and digestive.

Medicinal Uses: Relieves digestive issues, aids relaxation, and supports immune health.

Magical Uses: Purification, psychic powers, and enhancing spiritual clarity.

Identification: Lemongrass is an herb with long, slender leaves and a lemony fragrance. Harvesting: Cut the stalks close to the base.

Where to Find: Can be grown in gardens or purchased as dried leaves or essential oil.

Safety: Consult a healthcare professional before using medicinally, especially if pregnant or breastfeeding.

## Licorice Root

Properties: Soothing, anti-inflammatory, and promoting adrenal support.

Medicinal Uses: Supports digestive health, aids respiratory conditions, and soothes inflamed tissues.

Magical Uses: Enhancing love spells, promoting harmony, and attracting positive energies.

Identification: Licorice Root is a perennial herb with woody roots and sweet-tasting compounds.

Harvesting: Three to four years after growth is when the roots can be harvested.

Where to Find: Licorice Root can be purchased from herbal stores or online in dried form.

## Lilac

Properties: Fragrance, beauty, love, awakens the senses and healing.

Medicinal Uses: Destroys parasitic worms, treats skin problems and wounds, relieves toothaches, prevents bloating, promotes heart health, originally used for rheumatism and lowering insulin.

Magical Uses: Attracts love, romance, positive energy and spiritual growth. Enhances passion, promotes emotional healing, intuition, and spiritual awareness.

Identification: Clusters of fragrant, tubular flowers that belong to the many species of Syringa genus.

Harvesting: Flowers typically bloom in spring. Best to harvest them when they're in full bloom. Cut the flower clusters with sharp pruners or scissors, leaving enough stem to use them for various purposes.

Where to Find: Found in gardens and parks. They can also be bought at local flower shops or nurseries during their blooming season.

## Lotus Flower

Properties: Spiritual enlightenment, purity, tranquility.

Medicinal Uses: Has been used to boost overall immunity, improves mood, and libido.

Magical Uses: Meditation, spiritual rituals, invoking higher consciousness and enhances spiritual growth.

Identification: Lotus Flower is an aquatic plant with large, distinctive flowers in various colors.

Harvesting: Obtain lotus flowers or petals from trusted herbal suppliers.

Where to Find: Lotus flowers are native to Asia and can be found through specialized herbal suppliers.

Safety: Lotus flower is usually used in spiritual practices and not for medicinal purposes.

## Mandrake

Properties: Enchanting, hypnotic, and poisonous (all parts).

Medicinal Uses: Not recommended for medicinal use due to its toxicity, but has been used to treat stomach ulcers, hay fever, coughs, rheumatism and more.

Magical Uses: Attracts love, fertility and enhances magical rituals.

Identification: Mandrake is a perennial herb with large leaves and bell-shaped flowers, typically with a forked root.

Harvesting: Exercise extreme caution and consult experts; mandrake is highly toxic.

Where to Find: Specialty herbal stores and suppliers in dried form.


**Marigold**

Properties: Protection, prosperity, and promoting positive energy.

Medicinal Uses: Supports skin health, relieves inflammation, and aids wound healing.

Magical Uses: Warding off negative energies, attracting abundance, and enhancing divination.

Identification: Marigold is an annual or perennial herb with bright orange or yellow flowers.

Harvesting: Gather the flowers when they are fully open.

Where to Find: Marigold can be grown in gardens or purchased as dried flowers or herbal extracts.

## Mistletoe

Properties: Love, healing, and fertility.

Medicinal Uses: Used to support cardiovascular health, immunity boosting, and promotes relaxation.

Magical Uses: Associated with love, fertility, protection, transformation and healing. Used in spells and rituals related to romance, marriage, and attracting positive energy.

Identification: A parasitic plant that grows on the branches of trees, especially deciduous trees like oak, apple, and hawthorn. Has distinctive green leaves and clusters of small, white berries.

Harvesting: Requires caution and respect for the plant and its host tree, so neither is harmed. It's best to harvest during the Winter when it is easy to spot on bare trees.

Where to Find: Found in various regions, depending on the species and climate. Often available during the Winter or Holiday season in floral shops, craft stores, and specialty retailers.

**Mugwort**

Properties: Enhancing psychic abilities, protection, and dreamwork.

Medicinal Uses: Supports digestive health, aids menstruation, and has mild sedative properties.

Magical Uses: Divination, astral projection, and enhances psychic dreams.

Identification: A perennial herb with deeply lobed leaves and clusters of small flowers.

Harvesting: Gather the aerial parts (leaves and flowers) when the plant is in full bloom.

Where to Find: Can be found growing in fields, meadows, or herb gardens, or purchased from herbal stores.

Safety: Avoid using while pregnant or planning to become pregnant, as it can cause uterine contractions.

**Mullein**

Properties: Soothing, respiratory support, and protective.

Medicinal Uses: Relieves respiratory issues, soothes inflammation, and aids ear health.

Magical Uses: Protection, divination, and dream-work.

Identification: Mullein is a biennial herb with large fuzzy leaves and tall spikes of yellow flowers.

Harvesting: Gather the aerial parts (leaves and flowers) during the blooming season.

Where to Find: Can be found growing in fields, meadows, or herb gardens, or purchased from herbal stores.

## Neroli

Properties: Anti-fungal, soothing, naturally calming,

Medicinal Uses: Anti-inflammatory, stress and anxiety-relieving, antimicrobial, soothing for skin irritation

Magical Uses: Attracts good luck, love, creates a sense of joy and happiness, rids negative habits, thoughts, and feelings.

Identification: A pale-yellow essential oil derived from the flowers of bitter orange trees (citrus aurantium).

Harvesting: When the bitter orange tree flowers, you can harvest the blossoms for steam distillation to extract the oil

Where to Find: Found in Spain, Algeria, Italy, Egypt and other countries, from bitter orange trees. Easier to buy from special suppliers and can be purchased in oil form.

## Nutmeg

Properties: Warming, comforting, and aromatic.

Medicinal Uses: Relieves digestive issues, aids sleep, and has antimicrobial properties.

Magical Uses: Enhancing luck, protection, and attracting abundance.

Identification: Nutmeg is a spice derived from the seed of the Myristica fragrans tree.

Harvesting: Commercially available as dried spice.

Where to Find: Nutmeg can be purchased from grocery stores or spice suppliers.

## Orange

Properties: Uplifting, energizing, and associated with joy and creativity.

Medicinal Uses: Rich in vitamin C, supports immune health, and aids digestion.

Magical Uses: Attracts happiness, prosperity, and enhances creativity.

Identification: Orange is a citrus fruit with a bright orange color and a refreshing aroma.

Harvesting: Available as fresh fruit or as an essential oil.

Where to Find: Oranges can be purchased from grocery stores or herbal suppliers.

## Orris Root Powder

Properties: Enhancing love and romance, promoting psychic abilities, and attracting positivity.

Medicinal Uses: Not commonly used medicinally.

Magical Uses: Love spells, divination, and invokes the energy of Venus.

Identification: Orris Root Powder comes from the dried root of the Iris germanica plant.

Harvesting: Can be purchased from herbal stores or online.

Where to Find: Can be found in specialized herbal suppliers.

## Palo Santo

Properties: Purifying, grounding, and promoting spiritual clarity.

Medicinal Uses: Traditionally used for respiratory issues and relaxation.

Magical Uses: Cleansing rituals, enhances meditation, and spiritual protection.

Identification: Palo Santo is a tree native to South America, and the wood is used for its aromatic properties.

Harvesting: Palo Santo products, such as incense or essential oil, can be purchased from herbal or spiritual supply stores.

Where to Find: Can be purchased from herbal or spiritual supply stores.

## Passionflower

Properties: Calming, sedative, and promoting relaxation.

Medicinal Uses: Relieves anxiety, aids sleep, and supports nervous system health.

Magical Uses: Enhances dreamwork, promotes peace, and attracts love.

Identification: Passionflower is a climbing vine with intricate, colorful flowers.

Harvesting: Gather the aerial parts (leaves, stems, and flowers) when the plant is in full bloom.

Where to Find: Can be found growing in gardens or purchased as dried herbs or herbal supplements.

## Patchouli

Properties: Grounding, sensual, and attracting abundance.

Medicinal Uses: Not commonly used medicinally.

Magical Uses: Attracts love and wealth, enhances sensuality, and promotes grounding.

Identification: Patchouli is a perennial herb with fragrant, furry leaves.

Harvesting: Gather the leaves and stems when the plant is mature.

Where to Find: Can be grown in gardens or purchased as dried leaves or essential oil.

## Peppermint

Properties: Cooling, refreshing, and promoting digestion.

Medicinal Uses: Relieves digestive issues, aids headache relief, and supports respiratory health.

Magical Uses: Clears energy, enhances psychic abilities, and promotes clarity.

Identification: Peppermint is a perennial herb with serrated leaves and purple flowers.

Harvesting: Gather the aerial parts (leaves and flowers) when the plant is in full bloom.

Where to Find: Peppermint can be grown in gardens or purchased as dried leaves or essential oil.

## Poppy

Properties: Relaxing, sedative, and pain-relieving.

Medicinal Uses: Traditionally used for pain relief and promoting sleep.

Magical Uses: Enhances dreamwork, promotes relaxation, and invokes trance-like states.

Identification: Poppy is an annual or perennial herb with colorful flowers and distinctive seed pods.

Harvesting: Gather the aerial parts (leaves, stems, and flowers) after the petals have fallen.

Where to Find: Poppy seeds or extracts can be purchased from herbal stores or online.

## Raspberry Leaf

Properties: Nourishing, toning, and promoting reproductive health.

Medicinal Uses: Supports menstrual health, aids pregnancy, and promotes healthy digestion.

Magical Uses: Love spells, enhances fertility, and connects with feminine energy.

Identification: Raspberry Leaf is a shrub with prickly stems and clusters of white or pink flowers.

Harvesting: Gather the leaves before flowering or during the fruiting season.

Where to Find: Can be found growing in gardens or purchased as dried leaves or herbal tea.

## Rosemary

Properties: Refreshing, stimulates the senses and invigorates the mind.

Medicinal Uses: Stimulates memory and concentration, promotes mental clarity and alertness, aids in digestion, alleviates headaches. As it is a natural antioxidant, it can support overall well-being and immune health.

Magical Uses: Protective, wards off negative energies, promotes clarity, enhances mental focus, and used in rituals for remembrance and honoring loved ones who have passed on.

Identification: A woody-stemmed shrub with narrow, needle-shaped leaves. The plant produces small, pale blue flowers, that have a pleasant aroma.

Harvesting: Gently snip the young stems just above a leaf node. Avoid cutting too much from one plant to allow for healthy regrowth.

Where to Find: Can be found in gardens, herb nurseries, and in mild regions in the wild. It is also readily available in grocery stores and markets.

Safety: Pregnant individuals and those with epilepsy should avoid consuming large quantities of rosemary, since it can potentially stimulate the uterus or trigger seizures.

## Rue

Properties: Protective, warding off evil, and promoting purification.

Medicinal Uses: Traditionally used for digestive issues and as a natural insect repellent.

Magical Uses: Banishes negativity, protection, and enhances psychic abilities.

Identification: Rue is a perennial herb with bluish-green leaves and small yellow flowers.

Harvesting: Gather the aerial parts (leaves and flowers) when the plant is in full bloom.

Where to Find: Can be found growing in gardens or purchased as dried leaves or herbal extracts.

Safety: Exercise caution and avoid excessive use; rue can be toxic in large amounts.

**Saffron**

Properties: Mood-boosting, memory-enhancing, uplifting.

Medicinal Uses: Supports mood balance, aids digestion, libido, aids in relaxation, antioxidant.

Magical Uses: Enhances spell potency, protection, love spells, prosperity, wellness. Awakens psychic abilities, happiness.

Identification: Saffron is derived from the dried stigmas of the Crocus sativus flower.

Harvesting: Saffron threads are commercially available.

Where to Find: Can be purchased from specialty spice suppliers or herbal stores.

**Sage**

Properties: Cleansing, purifying, and protective.

Medicinal Uses: Supports respiratory health, soothes digestive discomfort. Antimicrobial and anti-inflammatory.

Magical Uses: Purifies and cleanse energies. Often used in smudging rituals to clear spaces, objects, and people of negative or stagnant energy. Enhances intuition, wisdom, and spiritual connection.

Identification: Refers to several different species of Salvia genus. Salvia officinalis, one of the most popular, has silvery-green leaves and produces small, tubular flowers in many colors.

Harvesting: Once plant has matured, leaves are carefully plucked. It's best to harvest leaves in the morning when its properties are most potent. Can be used fresh or dried for later use.

Where to Find: Grows in many regions worldwide. Can be found in grocery stores, herbal shops, and online suppliers. You can grow your own as well.

## Sandalwood

Properties: Grounding, purifying, and promoting spiritual awareness.

Medicinal Uses: Traditionally used for skin conditions, respiratory issues, and relaxation.

Magical Uses: Enhances meditation, promotes spiritual connection, and attracts positive energy.

Identification: Sandalwood is a fragrant tree with aromatic heartwood.

Harvesting: It is easier for most people to find sandalwood in the form of essential oil or incense.

Where to Find: Indigenous to India and Australia, or else in herbal or supply stores.

## Sassafras

Properties: Energizing, warming, and promoting circulation.

Medicinal Uses: Supports digestive health, aids menstrual discomfort, and has antimicrobial properties.

Magical Uses: Enhancing creativity, promoting positive energy, and attracting abundance.

Identification: Sassafras is a tree with distinctive lobed leaves and fragrant bark.

Harvesting: Available as dried leaves or bark, can be purchased from herbal stores.

Where to Find: Can be found through specialized herbal suppliers.

Safety: There are safety concerns around a compound called safrole, which can be a carcinogen. Thus, many manufacturers sell sassafras bark without this compound in it nowadays.

**Sea Salt**

Properties: Purifying, cleansing, and promoting protection.

Medicinal Uses: Believed to help increase hydration and blood pressure

Magical Uses: Cleansing rituals, protection spells, and banishing negativity.

Identification: Sea salt is obtained from evaporated seawater and looks like small white crystals clumped together.

Harvesting: Commercially available as coarse or fine crystals.

Where to Find: Can be purchased from grocery stores.

**Slippery Elm**

Properties: Soothing, healing, and promoting gastrointestinal health.

Medicinal Uses: Supports digestive health, aids sore throat, and soothes skin conditions.

Magical Uses: Enhances communication, promotes harmony, and attracts love.

Identification: Slippery Elm is a deciduous tree with rough bark and mucilaginous inner bark.

Harvesting: Can be purchased from herbal suppliers.

Where to Find: Slippery Elm bark can be found through specialized herbal suppliers.

## Spearmint

Properties: Cooling, good for digestion, and refreshing.

Medicinal Uses: Relieves indigestion, relieves nausea, supports respiratory health.

Magical Uses: Healing, enhances mental clarity, love, protection, attracts positive energy, and promotes healing.

Identification: A plant with bright green leaves and a sweet fragrance.

Harvesting: Gather the leaves just before the plant flowers.

Where to Find: Anywhere herbs grow wild, or from most stores in the form of dried leaves or herbal tea.

Safety: Generally safe, but may interfere with hormones, iron levels, and birth control pill effectiveness in large quantities.

## Spikenard

Properties: Spiritual transformation, protection, and devotion.

Medicinal Uses: Calming and grounding, aids in stress relief, promotes sleep, and emotional well-being. Antimicrobial and anti-inflammatory.

Magical Uses: Spiritual transformation, inner wisdom, protective, evokes a sense of sacred space, connects you to higher realms and divine energies, energetic protection, deepens meditation, and enhances devotion.

Identification: A flowering plant with long, thin stalks and small pink or purple flowers.

Harvesting: Typically harvested in the plant's second or third year of growth, once the roots have reached maturity.

Where to Find: Native to the Himalayas, the root and essential oil can be found in specialty herbal and health shops or online retailers.

**St. John's Wort:**

Properties: Mood-balancing, uplifting, and promoting emotional well-being.

Medicinal Uses: Supports mood balance, aids sleep, and relieves nerve pain.

Magical Uses: Protection, banishes negative energies, and enhances psychic abilities. Identification: St. John's Wort is a perennial herb with bright yellow flowers.

Harvesting: Gather the aerial parts (leaves, stems, and flowers) when the plant is in full bloom.

Where to Find: St. John's Wort can be found growing in fields, meadows, herb gardens, or purchased from herbal stores.

Safety: Consult a healthcare professional before using medicinally, especially if taking other medications. St. John's Wort can negatively interact with certain medications.

**Tobacco**

Properties: Stimulating, and relaxing.

Medicinal Uses: Originally used for pain relief, stress reduction, and aiding in relaxation.

Magical Uses: originally used for spiritual connection and communicating with ancestors. Can release negative energy and promote grounding.

Identification: A tall plant with large, green leaves and trumpet-shaped flowers.

Harvesting: Leaves are harvested once plant has fully grown and leaves have turned yellow-green.

Where to Find: Grown in many regions. Easily available as tobacco products like essential oil, or loose tobacco for smoking.

Safety: Be careful with tobacco. It can be harmful due to its addictive nature, and the risks of countless potential side effects when smoked.

## Vanilla

Properties: Calming, comforting, and aromatic.

Medicinal Uses: Soothes stomach issues, and reduces anxiety.

Magical Uses: Enhances love, desire, and passion. Inspires attraction, promotes comfort and relaxation.

Identification: Comes from pods of orchids, and has a sweet, rich smell.

Harvesting: Pods can be picked once they mature (turn dark brown or black).

Where to Find: Often available in most grocery stores as an extract or flavoring for cooking, and can be found in person or online.

Safety: Generally safe, but be careful about consuming large amounts of pure extract since it contains alcohol.

**Vervain**

Properties: Enhancing spiritual abilities, protection, and promoting clarity.

Medicinal Uses: Supports nervous system health, aids digestion, and relieves tension.

Magical Uses: Enhances spell work, promotes divine connection, and invokes spiritual protection.

Identification: Vervain is a perennial herb with small, delicate flowers and serrated leaves.

Harvesting: Gather the aerial parts (leaves and flowers) when the plant is in full bloom.

Where to Find: Can be found growing in fields, meadows, or herb gardens, or purchased from herbal stores.

**Vetiver**

Properties: Calms nervousness, helps muscle pain, repellent.

Medicinal Uses: Stress relief, calms muscle pain and cramps, promotes good sleep, bug repellent, used for stings and burns.

Magical Uses: Attracts money, enhances calmness and promotes peace, provides quality sleep, inspires love especially for same sex relationships, removes curses

Identification: A bunchgrass plant from the Poaceae family, a perennial plant

Harvesting: The roots can be harvested 18 - 24 months after it's planted.

Where to Find: Typically found in India, Indonesia and Sri Lanka. The oil is available in herbal and health stores that sell essential oils.

**Witch Hazel**

Properties: Astringent, soothing, and promoting skin health.

Medicinal Uses: Supports skin health, relieves inflammation, and aids wound healing.

Magical Uses: Protection, banishes negative energies, grief healing, and enhances divination.

Identification: Witch Hazel is a shrub with distinctive, spidery flowers and serrated leaves.

Harvesting: Gather the leaves and bark as needed.

Where to Find: Witch Hazel products, such as extracts or topical applications, can be purchased from herbal stores or specialty suppliers.

## Wolfsbane

Properties: Poisonous, protection against supernatural entities, associated with transformation.

Medicinal Uses: Not recommended for medicinal use due to its toxicity.

Magical Uses: Protection and banishment against negative energies, promotes transformation, anti-inflammatory, analgesic, anti-rheumatic, sedative

Identification: Wolfsbane is a perennial herb with distinctive blue or purple flowers.

Harvesting: Exercise extreme caution and avoid harvesting or using wolfsbane due to its extreme toxicity.

Where to Find: Can be found in mountain regions of Asia, Europe and North America, as well as specialty shops and suppliers.

## Wormwood

Properties: Enhances psychic abilities, protection, and promotes clarity.

Medicinal Uses: Traditionally used for digestive issues and as a natural insect repellent.

Magical Uses: Divination, spirit work, and enhances ritual practices.

Identification: Wormwood is a perennial herb with silvery-green foliage and small yellow flowers.

Harvesting: Gather the aerial parts (leaves and flowers) when the plant is in full bloom.

Where to Find: Can be found growing in fields, meadows, or herb gardens, or purchased from herbal stores.

Safety: Use caution and avoid excessive use; worm-wood produces thujone, which can be toxic in large amounts.

## Yarrow Flower

Properties: Protective, healing, and promoting psychic abilities.

Medicinal Uses: Supports wound healing, promotes liver function aids in cold and flu relief, and alleviates stomach issues like digestion.

Magical Uses: Love and marriage spells due to its ability to keep people together, protection, divination, and enhances spiritual energy

Identification: Yarrow is a perennial herb with feathery leaves and clusters of small, white or pink flowers.

Harvesting: Gather the aerial parts (leaves and flowers) when the plant is in full bloom.

Where to Find: Can be found growing in fields, meadows, or herb gardens, or purchased from herbal stores.

## Yellow Dock

Properties: Detoxifying, blood-cleansing, and promoting digestive health.

Medicinal Uses: Supports liver health, aids digestion, and promotes healthy elimination.

Magical Uses: Banishes negativity, protection, and promotes grounding.

Identification: Yellow Dock is a perennial herb with large, dock-like leaves and clusters of small flowers.

Harvesting: Gather the aerial parts (leaves, stems, and flowers) during the growing season.

Where to Find: Can be found growing in fields, meadows, or herb gardens, or purchased from herbal stores.

## Ylang Ylang

Properties: Renowned for its exotic fragrance and association with sensuality, love, and relaxation.

Medicinal Uses: Used in aromatherapy to promote a sense of calmness, reduce anxiety, and uplift mood. Believed to enhance sensuality and intimacy.

Magical Uses: Attracts love, enhances passion, and creates a harmonious atmosphere. Perfect for love spells, self-love rituals, etc

Identification: Scientifically called Cananga odorata, it's a tropical tree featuring fragrant, star-shaped flowers.

Harvesting: Typically harvested early in the morning when their aroma is at its peak.

Where to Find: Various tropical regions worldwide, like Indonesia, Madagascar, and the Philippines. As well, the essential oil and other Ylang Ylang products can be found in specialty stores, and herbal shops.

It's so important to dedicate time to doing your own research when it comes to herbs. They have so many amazing properties, uses, their potential effects, and any possible interactions. This is especially true if you intend to ingest herbs you are unfamiliar with. Some qualified experts include herbalists, healthcare professionals and longtime green witches. They can provide you with valuable insights and advice to ensure your experiences with herbs are always safe and beneficial.

# Chapter Seven

# Ritual Drawing Oils

Special, well-crafted mixtures blended from herbs, roots, and essential oils, have a long history that dates back to Ancient Egypt, perhaps even further still, to times immemorial. Those who work with this kind of magic find that the combinations of oils and herbs used inside ritual oils, which each possess their own frequency and magical properties, have both spiritual and magical effects in life. Essentially, ritual oils are just another way of creating changes in our lives, or the lives of others, using the energies found in nature - particularly in plants, roots, and oils.

There are five types of ritual oils, and each one serves a different purpose. These oil mixtures were known mainly as Hoodoo, Conjure, Anointing, Dressing, and Condition oils. However, these days people tend to classify them all as ritual oils, or else, they will use the five mixture types interchangeably.

For education's sake, this is a brief description of the five types and their purpose. Originally, Hoodoo oils were used in Black American folk magic to attract love, protection, wealth, and to break curses and hexes. Conjure oils serve as a means of communicating or paying homage to spiritual entities, or ancient gods and goddesses, as well as to protect against negative forces and provide healing - spiritually or physically. Anointing oils are often used to consecrate an individual or item, while Dressing oils are used on candles and other tools for spells. Lastly, Condition oils are commonly wiped onto items or areas to either attract energies or repel them.

Rootworkers, practitioners of Hoodoo, Voodoo, Wicca, and Green Witches often use these concoctions for anointing candles, anointing certain parts of the body, performing rituals, crafting spells, enchanting charms, and aromatherapy. Certain ritual oils can draw various things into your life such as love, success, healing, luck and more. In addition, sometimes ritual oils are used to attract spirits, to honor angels or demons, to astral travel, de-stress, for transformation or connect to those who have passed on from the physical world. There are literally hundreds of different types of ritual oils, and once you understand herbs and oils, and you set your intention, you can even craft your very own unique oils.

## How to Use Ritual Oils Correctly

Green witches use ritual oils in plenty of different ways depending on their desired outcome. As stated before, you can use them on the body - many people use love oils of various kinds on their body's when trying to attract someone, or confidence oils if they desire to become more confident for example. Alternatively, you may choose to have a ritual bath where you place a few drops of these special oils into your bathwater. Please note that before you apply any oil to your skin, it is important to dilute it first within a carrier oil in order to prevent any potential negative reactions. This is especially true if you have allergies or just sensitive skin in general. As well, personally, I do not recommend using cinnamon oil on your skin if you have sensitive skin, or at least do a patch test first. This is because it is known to be irritating. The powder or sticks may work better for you, if you choose to use them in your own ritual oils.

Additionally, ritual oils can be added to candles as part of spells or inserted into an oil burner and used for visualizations, meditations, and rituals. Some people put them on crystals, talismans, altars, and other items in order to infuse their work with magical energy.

To get you started on your ritual oil journey, I have provided you with a few of my personally crafted, and all-time favorite ritual oil blends. You will realize that they are not difficult to make, although it may feel intimidating at first. But as you get into it, I hope you will share my feelings and find the creation process to be a calming, therapeutic experience.

Once you have gathered all of your materials, I urge you to take your time, breathe deeply, and in a quiet space, or with some of your favorite, relaxing music playing in the background, choose a recipe from below.

### Ritual Oil Recipes

**Tools:** Before you begin any of the following ritual oil recipes you will need a glass bottle with a dropper.

**Directions:** After creating your mixture as instructed in the recipes, be sure to top off your glass bottle with a carrier oil of your choice. You can use jojoba oil, avocado oil, sweet almond oil, apricot kernel oil, sweet almond oil, sunflower oil, or olive oil. Other oil options are possible as well, but try to avoid oils like coconut oil, which will solidify at room temperature, and canola oil, which is heavily processed. Jojoba oil will help your mixture last the longest, but vegetable oils are the cheapest.

Don't fill up your bottle to the very top, as your bottle's dropper may push out some of the oil when you close the bottle, causing spillage.

Once your bottle is tightly capped, you will want to draw out the essences of the essential oils, roots and/or herbs you used in your mixture. You can achieve this in two ways.

The first way is to simply find a cool, dark place to store your ritual oil blend for the next two to four weeks. During this time, herbs and/or roots that you use in your mixture will naturally be infused into the carrier oil.

The second way is much faster, but takes a little more work. It involves the double-boiling technique. This is an ancient way in which people have infused oils with natural substances. The idea is that the heat from the boiling water will delicately warm up your ritual oil mixture, drawing out the essence of your ingredients, and ultimately getting the most potency out of each component without damaging the properties.

Practitioners of this method believe that this procedure effectively helps to unlock the purest form of any herb or oil's essence, making it even more effective.

**Step 1**

You will need a large pot, as well as a glass cup that can withstand high temperatures. I normally use a glass measuring cup, due to its durability and thickness.

**Step 2**

Fill the glass cup halfway with water. Then place your glass bottle containing your mixture inside it. Fill the larger pot halfway with water, and place the measuring cup inside that pot. Make sure the water does not overflow.

**Step 3**

Turn the stove up to high heat until the water begins to boil in the pot.

Eventually, the water inside the glass cup will begin to boil as well. Turn the heat down to low, and allow the water to simmer.

After about 10 - 15 minutes, remove your bottled ritual oil from the heat. *Be careful!* The bottle may be very hot at this point. The coolest part of your bottle will be the tip of the dropper lid, and thus the part you will want to touch when you are ready to remove it from the water.

Allow your ritual oil to cool before use. Label, date if possible, and store in a cool, dry place.

**For Longer Lasting Oils:**

- Use Jojoba oil because it will help your mixture stay fresh the longest.

- Add a few drops of Vitamin E oil to your mixture when finished because this acts as a natural preservative which will help your ritual oil stay fresh for a long time as well.

- Never use plants, herbs or roots in your mixtures unless you know they are completely dried. If they are not dried properly, they can potentially rot and spoil your oil.

## Making Your Ritual Oil Your Own

You can customize the recipes in this book or create your own versions of them, by adding drops of additional oils to the recipes or by replacing certain ingredients with others that you prefer. However, when you are adding or replacing ingredients, choose only those that align with the purpose of the ritual oil.

If you own mica powders, you can add a pinch of your chosen color to your ritual oil and it will create a gorgeous color within your blend.

## How to Apply Ritual Oils

Usage:

1. Set your intention for your oil, and the favorable outcome you desire, depending on its intended use. Ex. Love oil = I want to attract a loving relationship, Good luck = I want to attract good luck into my life

2. Go into a quiet, comfortable space where you can focus your energy, feel calm and connect with the energies around you.

3. Rub a few drops of your oil between your palms to activate its energies.

4. Close your eyes and deeply inhale the aroma, envisioning yourself surrounded by a vibrant aura of positive energy.

5. Apply a small amount of the oil to your body, or anoint the belongings that you wish to affect, or that represent the things you wish to affect in your life.

6. As you apply the oil, visualize yourself attracting positive opportunities, then feel confident and supported by the Universe, be-

cause you are.

7. End the ritual with gratitude, expressing thanks for the wonderful things that are now manifesting in your life.

Remember that any ritual's power does not rely solely on the ingredients you use, but also in your intentions and beliefs. Don't question or doubt this magic or your abilities, as this weakens magic. Be confident that all you want is already done, and release and let go of it and return to your life as usual. You may want to do something fun to take your mind off your ritual, or wind down with a good movie, show, song, etc. Your desires are on their way, trust this and you will see them in your 3D reality soon enough.

# Chapter Eight

# Magical Crafts

Now that you are more familiar with a wider range of herbs and oils and their magical properties, there are several magical items you can create at home as a new green witch, in order to bring the magic of nature into your daily life.

The benefit of creating your own homemade magical items is that they are infused with your unique intentions, personal energy, connection to nature, and intentions. The items are more powerful as a result of being specially attuned to you, for your personal use. Allow your intuition to guide you while you are crafting, and each time you use these items. And, of course, most importantly, make sure you are having fun along the way.

## *Creating Incense*

# Chapter Nine

# Culinary Conjuring

**D**rawing Your Intentions Into Your Life With Food!

Because we eat every day, many of us quite mindlessly, you may not think that there's any magic in food. But this could not be further from the truth. Any, and all foods can be used in green witchcraft. Why? Because all foods come from our Mother Earth, and Earth, itself, is magic.

We may not realize it all the time, but we are always using foods in our spells and rituals, and as offerings to our ancestors or to deities, as well as for healing. To most of the sleeping masses, food is simply another word for a snack, dish or meal. But, when you allow yourself to think about it further, you realize that all dishes can be broken down into single ingredients. And that all, if not most, of the ingredients come from nature. This includes anything from fruits and vegetables to grains, herbs, water, roots, seeds, etc. Each one holds a particular frequency or energy, which matches the frequency of certain properties. For instance, scientific studies have shown that bananas increase our serotonin levels. And similarly, in witchcraft bananas are indeed associated with happiness and elevated mood.

When we combine foods together to make a meal, we further increase the power of those foods as we infuse our own energies into our cooking. This is why it is so important to be intentional with every meal you make, because your personal energy is infused in everything you do.

Why do you think people love to say, "I love my mom's home-cooked meals." Anyone can make a baked mac n' cheese, but no one can make it like mom. Why is that? It's because mothers don't simply cook a meal like a cook at a restaurant; they infuse all their love, protection and connection to us into every meal they make. The same goes, of course, for any loving family member who cooks for us. We feel their love for us in each bite. While each food possesses certain properties, it's important to keep in mind our intentions.

Why are you making this meal? *Because you're hungry? Because you're celebrating? Because you're grieving?*

Who is going to eat it? *You? Family? Friends? A pet? Your workmates? Neighbors? Strangers?*

How do you want the food to make them feel? *Satisfied? Healthy? Comforted? Nourished?*

Ask yourself these kinds of questions while you prepare meals, until it comes naturally to you. Eventually, you will do it subconsciously. And watch the magical effects booking with intention has upon your meals, and those who delight in it.

In this section, we will briefly go over some foods and dishes that you can eat in our to draw your intentions into your life, effortlessly. In order to do this, simply think about your desired outcome as you chew. Take time to focus on each bite, breathe in the aroma of your meal, and feel yourself full of gratitude, knowing that your intentions have already manifested and are on their way to you.

**Good luck:** Eat pizza when you need some good luck in your life, and for success and courage. Pizza is associated with victory! Sports teams often celebrate their victories with pizza dinners. Hence, eating pizza will put you in a winner's mindset. And your reality will reflect those feelings back at you through amazing opportunities and good luck.

**Victory:** Ice-cream! Similar to pizza, ice-cream is associated with celebrations. And most importantly with winning. Children often receive ice-cream as a reward for accomplishing things. So eating ice-cream helps to align us with the energies of winning and achieving.

**Romance & Lust:** Want to inspire desire and lust in someone or yourself? Eat spaghetti. Spaghetti is a staple in Italian cuisine, and the idea of the passionate Italian lover is alive and well for good reason. Spaghetti sauce is made of plenty of herbs, and spices in a tomato base, which is known for its aphrodisiac properties. Basil is known for increasing sexual energy, as is garlic powder, and oregano is love-drawing. Together this meal creates the perfect food love spell.

**Happiness:** Apple pie! Apples have plenty of positive properties, one of which includes evoking feelings of happiness. Cinnamon is also great for happiness; eating a dish that blends the two is a surefire way to boost your mood.

**Lust:** Double dark chocolate cookies. Dark chocolate is not only healthy for you and good for your heart, but it is known to naturally increase libido. Have a rich dark chocolate dessert with someone you fancy the next time you see them!

**Money:** Coleslaw is a refreshing salad that also draws money and abundance thanks to ingredients like cabbage.

Onion rings are also a great option, or any dish that contains onions, really, as they happen to be money-drawing.

**Healing:** Mashed potatoes are known for their healing properties, making them an easy choice when you want to draw health into your life through the magic of food.

**Abundance:** Charcuterie boards represent abundance and variety, due to the diverse array of foods each board is made of. Cheese represents transformation, nourishment, and connection to the earth. Each type of cheese can carry its own magical qualities. For instance, a creamy Brie may symbolize sensuality and indulgence, while a sharp Cheddar can be linked to grounding and stability. Nuts are associated with wisdom, prosperity, and manifestation. Each type of nut carries its own unique energy. Almonds can symbolize fertility and good fortune, while walnuts can be linked to grounding and protection. Crackers like water crackers represent clarity and focus.

*Here is a breakdown of different foods that also have magic associations. Keep in mind that this list is short compared to all the foods out there that can be used in your kitchen witchcraft.*

Apples: Apples are also associated with happiness, fertility, and healing in witchcraft.

Apricots: Attracts love and are often used in love spells in the form of apricot oil.

Avocado: Associated with stamina, fertility, virility and female health. Consume whenever you need an energy boost; perfect for outside and inside the bedroom.

Bananas: Happiness, mood-boosting, lust-inducing and protection.

Bagel: Represents wholeness, unity, and the cyclical nature of life. Bagels are often used in rituals for protection, attracting blessings, and promoting a sense of completeness or fulfillment. Sesame seeds are money-drawing, so you can eat a sesame seed bagel to attract wealth.

Bread: Symbolizes sustenance, nourishment, and grounding. It is often used in rituals and spells related to abundance, prosperity, and stability. Sharing bread is also a gesture of community and unity. Whole-grain bread is associated with grounding.

Carrots: Carrots have long been associated with fertility and lust, due to their deep color (orange, purple, etc.) and their shape.

Chocolate: Chocolate is a delicious food that lovers give each other on holidays, and it has a long-standing history of being associated with love. Draw on the energies of love by biting into a piece of chocolate when you wish to invite it into your life. Eat chocolate, or treats like strawberries dipped in chocolate to attract love and romance. As well, Aztecs and Mayans consumed chocolate in order to increase their warrior classes' vitality, virility, power and stamina. Eating milk chocolate attracts friendship and support. At the same time, dark chocolate is an amazing aphrodisiac.

Cinnamon: Symbolizes passion, success, and spiritual growth. It is often used in food when you wish to enhance love, attract abundance, and increase personal power.

Coffee:  Associated with energy, stimulation, and focus. Coffee is perfect to consume to enhance mental clarity, focus, increase your productivity, and promotes vitality. Coffee is also used for divination and to amplify one's psychic abilities.

Fruit: All fruit attract abundance, fertility, and healing into your life. So get your fill of fruit; you really cannot go wrong.

Garlic: Garlic banishes negative energies, and unwanted influences, also possesses protective properties.

Honey: Symbolizes sweetness, love, and attraction. It is often used in spells related to love, harmony, and prosperity.

Hot peppers: Hot peppers are excellent for attracting weight loss, as it boosts your metabolism. It also promotes stamina and increases your energy as well. It is used for healing because hot peppers increase circulation throughout the body, which is good for overall health.

Lettuce: Eat lettuce for healing and divination.

Maple Syrup: Use maple syrup in your food, swapping out white processed sugar for it, and draw money and love into your life.

Oats: Oats and other grains like barley, etc., are money-drawing, healing, and nourishing.

Onion: Onions are great to consume to draw money into your life, health, lust and protection.

Orange: Associated with increasing your energy and boosting your mood.

Pasta: Protection, creativity and connection.

Plantain: Attracts strength, protection and healing. It is believed that hanging a plantain leaf in your car protects you from accidents, and in my own experience consuming cooked, ripe plantain aids in reducing digestive issues and stomach problems.

Pumpkin: Symbolizes prosperity, abundance, and protection. It is often used in rituals during the harvest season and for manifestation spells.

Rice: Rice is associated with protection, abundance, and lust.

Rum (and other spirits): Ideal offering to deities, ancestors, gods, and goddesses, good for divination and when you want to channel spirits as well. Use it in your dishes, like in the tomato paste of pasta or spaghetti for a romantic and fun night, or, in desserts like rum cake, cream soda or hot chocolate with a shot of rum.

Sea salt: Consume salt for protection and purification. The best salt is Celtic sea salt because it retains the most minerals that our bodies desperately need.

Strawberries: Eat strawberries to attract romance, love, sensuality, and fertility. Keep in mind that love also refers to self-love, so fixing yourself a healthy and delicious bowl is a beautiful way of displaying self-love.

Sugar: Happiness, energy, and kindness, as it is often used in spellwork to "sweeten up" your target.

Watermelon: Watermelon is known for its aphrodisiac effects as well as for its energy-boosting and healing properties.

Zucchini: Zucchinis are associated with prosperity and protection. Make zucchini fritters or zucchini brownies to infuse them with these amazing properties.

## Tea Recipes

### *Love Drawing Tea*

For: Love, Happy, Money

Love drawing tea is a wonderful way to attract more love into your life, whether that be romantic love, love for friends and family, or self-love. Here's a soothing, unique and delicious blend of herbs and spices that heavily attracts love to the drinker.

Ingredients:

- 2 cups of water

- 1 cinnamon stick (or 1 teaspoon ground cinnamon)

- 1 tsp grated fresh ginger (or ½ teaspoon ground ginger)

- 1 tbsp dried damiana leaves

- 1 vanilla pod (or 1 teaspoon pure vanilla extract)

- 1 tbsp dried rose petals

Serves: 2

Instructions:

1. Begin by preparing your ingredients. If using a cinnamon stick, break it into smaller pieces to release the flavor. If using a vanilla pod, slice it lengthwise to expose the seeds.

2. In a small saucepan, add 2 cups of water and bring it to a gentle boil.

3. Reduce the heat to low, so that the water cools to a simmer.

4. Add the cinnamon, ginger, damiana, vanilla,

and rose petals to the water, allowing it to simmer for about 10 minutes. This helps the flavors to infuse. If desired, add your favorite milk to your mix. It can be nut milk, soy milk, or animal-based milk.

5. After simmering, remove the saucepan from the heat and let the tea steep for an additional 5 minutes.

6. Strain the tea to remove the solid ingredients, and pour it into teacups or a teapot.

7. If desired, sweeten your tea with honey, maple syrup or your preferred sweetener.

Enjoy the aroma and incredible flavor. With every sip, keep your intentions in mind by visualizing them and feeling gratitude towards their fulfillment.

Feel free to experiment with the quantities of ingredients, and adjust the flavor as you see fit, according to your preferences. Tea spells, like other spells, are a personal experience, so don't hesitate to modify the recipe to suit your taste better.

### *Happy Tea*

For: Happiness, health, connection, and bonding

This refreshing recipe is an uplifting iced tea you can drink anytime you need a quick mood-boost!

Ingredients:

- 4 cups water

- 4 cinnamon sticks

- 1 orange zest

- Juice of 2 oranges

- 2 tbsps -  honey or sweetener of your choice

- 2-3 star anise pods

- Ice cubes

- Orange slices (for garnish)

Serves approximately 4.

Instructions:

1. In a medium-sized saucepan, bring the water to a simmer.

2. Add the cinnamon sticks, orange zest, orange juice, honey (or sweetener), and star anise pods to the simmering water.

3. Allow the mixture to simmer for about 10 minutes to further infuse the flavors.

4. Next, remove your pan from the heat entirely, and allow the tea to stand and cool further.

5. Once your tea has cooled, strain the tea to remove the solid ingredients, such as the cinnamon sticks, orange zest, and star anise pods.

6. Transfer the tea to a pitcher and refrigerate for at least 1-2 hours to chill.

7. Once you are ready to serve, fill your glasses with ice cubes and pour chilled tea over it.

8. Want to be fancy? Add a slice of orange to each glass as a garnish. Stir gently and enjoy your refreshing, mood-boosting iced tea!

This flavorful and invigorating beverage is perfect for those hot days when you need a refreshing pick-me-up. Adjust the tea's sweetness to your personal tastes by adding more or less sweetener.

### *Warming Tea*

For: Warming, circulation, mood-boosting, and abundance

This tea will keep you warm on those cold Winter days, while lifting your spirits and promoting abundance!

Ingredients:

- 2 cups water

- 1 tbsp dried sassafras root bark

- 1 tbsp dried or fresh ginger

- 4 pieces of clove

- 1 piece of cinnamon stick or 1/2 tsp cinnamon powder

- 1 tsp honey or sweetener of your choice (optional)

- Milk (optional)

Serves: 2

Instructions:

1. Bring a small pot of water to a boil.

2. Add the sassafras root bark to the boiling water. Add the ginger and cinnamon.

3. Reduce the heat to low, allowing the tea to simmer for about 15- 20 minutes so the flavors can infuse with the water.

4. Next, remove the pan from heat.

5. Strain the tea to separate the ingredients from the liquid.

6. At this point, add your preferred type of milk, whether dairy or non-dairy, and stir.

7. Add your preferred sweetener as well, stirring until dissolved.

8. You can reheat the tea slightly if it has cooled too much from the milk.

9. Pour the tea into teacups and serve hot!

10. Enjoy the bold, warming flavors that perfectly meld together, the rich aroma, and experience your body heat up from the inside out!

All the ingredients have a warming effect on the body, which makes this the perfect Winter drink. However, warming herbs often help relax the body as well, so they can be consumed anytime you wish to wind down and destress.

## Calm Cycle Tea

For: Calming painful menstrual cramps, helps with digestion, warming,

This tea will keep your stomach calm and relaxed during your cycle, so that you don't have to suffer from painful cramps. There is no reason that women, and non-binary and afab people should have to deal with pain each month. Once again, nature provides us with solutions.

Ingredients:

- 2 cups water

- 1 tbsp dried Raspberry Leaf

- 1 tsp of chamomile

- 1 tbsp dried or fresh ginger

- 1 tsp fennel (optional)

- ¼ tsp anise (optional)

- 1 piece of cinnamon stick or 1/2 tsp cinna-mon powder (optional)

Serves: 2

Instructions:

1. Bring a small pot of water to a boil.

2. Add the ingredients to the boiling water.

3. Reduce the heat to low, allowing the tea simmer for about 10- 15 minutes so the flavors can infuse with the water.

4. Next, remove the pan from heat.

5. Strain the tea to separate the ingredients from the liquid.

6. Pour the tea into teacups and serve hot!

Experiment with the "optional" ingredients, adding a different one each time you make this tea, and see what kind of effect it has on your particular PMS symptoms.

All the ingredients have a calming effect on PMS symptoms, especially painful cramps. Drink as needed, but be careful not to consume too much ginger in one day, as that may have the opposite effect. All the ingredients can be consumed alone, as individual teas, so definitely experiment, especially if taste is an issue for you. This tea is more about its calming effects and less about tasting good. Still, you are free to add a sweetener or a bit of non-dairy tea if desired. Dairy is not recommended during menstrual cycles as it can irritate the stomach further.

### *Heart's Delight Tea*

For: Happiness, heart health, passion, psychic abilities

This revitalizing tea is not only a delicious drink you can enjoy hot or old, but its powerful ingredients like hawthorn and hibiscus, make it heart-healthy and anti-inflammatory too!

Ingredients:

- 2 cups water

- 1 tbsp dried hawthorn berries

- 1 tbsp dried hibiscus petals

- 1 tsp honey or sweetener of your choice (optional)

- Lemon slices or fresh mint leaves for garnish (optional)

Serves: 2

Instructions:

1. Bring some water to a boil inside a small pan.

2. Add the dried hawthorn berries and hibiscus petals to the boiling water.

3. Reduce the heat to low, allowing the tea simmer for about 10-15 minutes so the flavors can infuse with the water.

4. Once your tea has simmered, you can remove the pan from heat. Allow the tea to steep for another 5 minutes.

5. Finally, strain the tea to separate the hawthorn berries and hibiscus petals from the tea.

6. If desired, add honey or your preferred sweetener to taste and stir until dissolved.

7. You can pour the tea into teacups and enjoy it hot. Or chill it in the fridge for about an hour, and pour it into glasses over ice.

8. Garnish your drink with lemon slices, or fresh mint leaves for a nice, extra touch of flavor and aroma.

Because both hawthorn and hibiscus are known for their potential cardiovascular benefits, you never have to feel guilty about enjoying a drink so delicious. Its beautiful, rich color alone makes it tempting to try. Pair this flavorful tea with romance or lust-drawing foods to take advantage of all the health benefits and magical properties in a single meal! You can always adjust the sweetness of this tea depending on how you prefer it.

### Lovely Detox Tea

For: Detox, healing

This tea is ideal for anytime you wish to let go of toxins and waste in the body. Allows you to feel healthier and lighter.

Ingredients:

- 2 cups water

- 1 tbsp dried dandelion

- 1 tbsp dried wormwood

- 1/2 tsp yellow dock (dried, powdered, or fresh)

Serves: 3

Instructions:

1. Bring a small pot of water to a boil.

2. Add the ingredients to the boiling water.

3. Reduce the heat to low, allowing the tea simmer for about 10 - 15 minutes so the flavors can infuse with the water.

4. Next, remove the pan from heat.

5. Strain the tea to separate the ingredients from the liquid.

6. Pour the tea into teacups and serve hot!

7. Enjoy your detox tea, and with every sip, envision toxins clearing out from every cell in your body. Drink this tea 1 - 3 times daily for 8 - 10 days.

All the ingredients have detox properties, as well as being anti-inflammatory, and dandelion leaf aids with digestion. All the ingredients can be consumed alone, as individual teas, so definitely experiment, especially if taste is an issue for you. This tea focuses largely on the positive health benefits, not so much on flavor.

Adding sugar or dairy milk to this tea is not recommended, as these ingredients have the opposite effect of detoxing. Instead, pair this tea with a clean, healthy diet full of fresh fruit, and vegetables, and at least one salad per day. Avoiding meat and limiting the amount of cooked, fried, and processed food in your diet will help you get the most out of this tea blend.

### *Abundance Chocolate Tea*

For: Abundance, happiness, energy, love, circulation, success

There's something so special, so luxurious about the taste of real, authentic chocolate in recipes. Real chocolate has a certain creamy sweetness to it that perfectly contrasts its slight smokiness. This drink is inspired by the Jamaican "Chocolate Tea," and because of all the amazing herbs in this blend, it is also mood-boosting, promotes energy, and is abundance-drawing, so you can drink it anytime you desire to feel happier, increase your energy, and bring abundance into your life!

Ingredients:

- 2 cups water

- 2 cups of milk of your choice

- 3 Jamaican chocolate balls (grated) or ½ cup

of raw chocolate (grated)

- 1 tbsp of cinnamon powder or 1 cinnamon stick

- 5 tbsps or ⅓ cup of the sweetener of your choice (sweetened condensed milk, honey, maple syrup, sugar, etc.)

- ½ tsp vanilla extract

- ½ tsp allspice

- ¼ tsp ground nutmeg

- 1 cinnamon leaf (optional)

Serves: 2 - 4

Instructions:

1. Add water to a medium-sized saucepan.

2. Add your cinnamon stick and bring the pot of water to a boil.

3. Add your grated chocolate, allspice, ground nutmeg, and cinnamon leaf if you use it, to

the boiling water.

4. Reduce the heat to low, allowing the mixture to simmer for about 10 minutes so the flavors can infuse with the water.

5. Next, remove the pan from heat.

6. Stir in your milk and keep the lid on as you let it stand for another 10 minutes.

7. Strain the tea to separate the ingredients from the liquid.

8. Stir in your chosen sweetener.

9. When you are ready to drink, reheat slightly, then pour the tea into cups and serve hot!

Enjoy the aroma and incredible flavor. With every sip, keep your intentions in mind by visualizing them and feeling gratitude towards their fulfillment.

### *ImmuniTea*

For: Healing, relieving the symptoms of colds, immunity-boosting

This tea is perfect for whenever you feel a cold coming on, or if you simply wish to strengthen your immunity during those cold Autumn and Winter days.

Ingredients:

- 2 cups water

- 1 tbsp of lemongrass

- 1 tbsp of elderberries

- 1 tbsp of mint

- ¼ tsp anise

Serves 2

Instructions:

1. Add water to a small saucepan.

2. Bring the water to a boil.

3. Add your elderberries, mint, and lemongrass.

4. Reduce the heat to low, allowing the mixture to simmer for about 10 minutes so the healing ingredients can infuse with the water.

5. Next, remove the pan from heat.

6. When you are ready to drink, strain the tea into cups and serve hot!

7. You can add a squeeze of lemon to further boost the healing properties of this tea, or add a touch of raw honey to help soothe a sore throat and add a more pleasant taste.

Enjoy the aroma and incredible flavor. Keep your healing intentions in mind with every sip by visualizing your body growing stronger and more robust. Feel gratitude towards nature for providing us with such amazing, healing herbs.

### *Dreamtime Tea*

For: Lucid dreams, astral travels, psychic growth, divination, more insight into situations

Did you know that we travel to the astral plane and beyond in our astral bodies when we are asleep? It's no wonder that ancient people would wish each other "safe travels" before going to sleep.

But what if you could be more present, more conscious, and more intentional during your travels? That is what this tea was designed to do. This tea promotes astral travel, as well as lucid dreams - the dreams where you are aware that you are dreaming and you can control them. Astral travel and lucid dreaming are essential to our spiritual growth. They help us better understand ourselves and our purpose, solve problems in our lives, and our reality as a whole. Some people use it to connect to their guides, spirit families and to access other realms. Drink this tea before bed, or before a meditation session, whenever you want to explore more of the non-physical world and better understand yourself as a spiritual being.

Ingredients:

- 2 cups water

- 1 tbsp of dried lotus flower or jasmine flower

- 1 tbsp of mugwort

- 1 tbsp of orange peel

- ¼ tsp anise

Serves 2

Instructions:

1. Add water to a small saucepan.

2. Bring the water to a boil.

3. Add your ingredients to the water.

4. Reduce the heat to low, allowing the mixture to simmer for about 10 minutes, so that the herbal blend can infuse with the water.

5. Next, remove the pan from heat.

6. When you are ready to drink, strain the tea into cups and serve hot! Alternatively, you can chill your tea, mix in a sweetener and pour over ice for an iced version on those hot summer nights.

When using this tea, you may also wish to get a dream journal. Each time you are finished with a meditation session, or have just awoken after drinking this tea, write down whatever you experienced or can remember. Where did you go? What did you see? Who did you speak to? What did they say? Later, you can try interpreting the meaning of your experience. This practice will also help you to naturally get better at lucid dreaming as well.

Enjoy the aroma and incredible flavor. With every sip, keep your healing intentions in mind by visualizing your body growing stronger. Feel gratitude towards nature for providing us with such amazing, healing herbs.

### *Iron Tummy Tea*

For: Relief from indigestion and other stomach issues. Helps your tummy feel like new.

This tea is ideal for whenever you are experiencing stomach discomfort like indigestion, nausea, flatulence or just pain. This tea will make your stomach feel good as new, as if it was made of iron!

Ingredients:

- 2 cups water

- 1 tbsp peppermint

- 1 tsp of ginger

- 1 tbsp of lemongrass

- ¼ tsp anise (optional)

- ¼ tsp of cayenne (optional)

Serves: 2

Instructions:

1. Add water to a small saucepan.

2. Bring the water to a boil.

3. Add your ingredients.

4. Reduce the heat to low, allowing the mixture to simmer for about 10 minutes so the healing ingredients can infuse with the water.

5. Next, remove the pan from heat.

6. When you are ready to drink, strain the tea into cups and serve hot!

7. You can add a squeeze of lemon to further boost the healing properties of this tea, or add a touch of raw honey to help soothe

your stomach further and add a more pleasant taste.

The recipe lists anise and cayenne as options, but they are highly recommended for their amazing properties. What you may want to do is experiment with one of these ingredients when making your tea, and then try the other ingredient the next time you make it, and observe how you feel. You can also just try the two of them together in your tea, along with the other ingredients to see how they work with your particular issues. Make a note of what makes you feel best for next time!

Enjoy the aroma and incredible flavor. With every sip, keep your healing intentions in mind by visualizing your stomach feeling great! Feel gratitude towards nature for providing us with such amazing, healing herbs.

### *Relax Me Tea*

For: Relaxing, and relieving stress.

This tea is perfect to drink whenever you are stressed or anxious, and wish to relax.

Ingredients:

- 2 cups water

- 1 tbsp chamomile leaf

- ¼ tsp of passionflower

- ½ tsp of damiana leaf (optional)

Serves: 2

Instructions:

1. Add water to a small saucepan.

2. Bring the water to a boil.

3. Add your ingredients.

4. Reduce the heat to low, allowing the mixture to simmer for about 10 minutes so the healing ingredients can infuse with the water.

5. Next, remove the pan from heat.

6. When you are ready to drink, strain the tea into cups and serve hot!

7. Be sure to drink this mixture in a place where

you can relax, and where you do not need to operate machinery, drive, etc. This is because this mixture can make you so relaxed that you may feel sleepy! Take this drink to bed, or relax with it on the couch after a long day.

Enjoy the aroma and incredible flavor. With every sip, keep your intentions in mind by visualizing all stress and anxiety leaving your body! Feel gratitude towards nature for providing us with such amazing, healing herbs.

### *Hottie Tea*

For: Beauty and Health, boosts skin collagen, promotes healthy skin, promotes healthy weight, calming, stress-relieving, protection, peace, love

This tea promotes attractiveness in the drinker. The ingredients possess properties that aid in healthy skin, and a healthy metabolism. Drink this tea whenever you want to feel like you are doing something kind and loving for yourself, while making yourself even more attractive than you already are, both inside and out!

Ingredients:

- 2 cups water

- 1 tbsp calendula

- 1 tbsp of hibiscus

- Sweetener to taste (optional)

Serves: 2

Instructions:

1. Add water to a small saucepan.

2. Bring the water to a boil.

3. Add your ingredients.

4. Reduce the heat to low, allowing the mixture to simmer for about 10 minutes so the healing ingredients can infuse with the water.

5. Next, remove the pan from heat.

6. When you are ready to drink, strain the tea into cups and serve hot!

7. You can add a sweetener of your choice or

squeeze of lemon further boost the healing properties of this tea.

8. Try this tea iced! Simply chill this tea after removing from pan, then sweeten it and pour in glass over ice for a refreshing drink in the summer heat!

Enjoy the aroma and incredible flavor. With every sip, keep your healing intentions in mind by visualizing your body and skin looking and feeling amazing! Imagine yourself feeling peaceful and cared for, because self-care is so underrated yet so important in our lives. Feel gratitude towards nature for providing us with such amazing, healing herbs.

### *Pearly Whites Tea*

# Solstice and Equinox Rituals

For green witches, there is deep significance in honoring the equinoxes and solstices. You see, these pivotal times in each year are the very foundation of the witch's calendar. They serve to illuminate the changing seasons, while connecting us to the natural flows of the planet. Imagine you are standing at the threshold of a solstice or equinox. These sacred moments act as gateways, where the energy of the Universe converges, offering us a unique chance to align ourselves with the rhythm of life's cycles. Whether you're basking in the warmth of the summer solstice, or you're embracing the introspection of the winter solstice, each moment carries its own alluring magic.

During the solstices, the sun rises to its highest point and dips to its lowest point while it moves across the sky. The equinoxes, however, bring extraordinary balance to the days and nights, as they stand equal to each other. There are several benefits to working with these sacred moments in the year. For instance, when we work with them, we deepen our connection to nature. Another benefit to working with the equinoxes and solstices, we honor them and we attune ourselves to the Earth's natural cycles, which puts us more in line with its rhythms. This connection creates a sense of grounding, balance, and the feeling of being rooted in the world around us. Also, embracing these celestial events empowers us to live in harmony with the cosmos. When we align our spell work and intentions with the solstices and equinoxes, we are able to connect to the incredible forces of life, amplifying the results of our magic. This harmony also brings us clarity, wisdom, direction, and the opportunity to grow spiritually. Additionally, we can honor our ancestors by following their traditional observances of the equinoxes and solstices, and working with them. It is a way to close the divide between ancient practices and the modern era, to pay tribute to our ancestors who celebrated these events in times long gone, and to find insight and direction in the old ways.

Lastly, the equinoxes and solstices gift us with powerful energies that we can harness to help us in our own transformations and manifestations. These sacred moments provide potent portals for setting intentions, releasing what no longer serves us, and bringing our desires into our physical reality.

## Winter Solstice Ritual

The Winter Solstice marks the time of year with the shortest days and subsequently the longest nights. Hence, many green witches like to celebrate the Winter Solstice because it represents the sun's return, the welcoming of light and the rebirth of nature.

Materials You Will Need:

- White candle (representing the returning sun)

- Evergreen branches or wreaths

- Matches or a lighter

- Blankets or warm clothing

Instructions:

1. Find a quiet space indoors or outdoors where you can perform this ritual undisturbed.

2. Set up your ritual space, placing the white candle in the center while the evergreen branches or wreaths are arranged around it.

3. Light the candle, and focus on its flame. View it as a representation of the returning of light to the Earth.

4. Next, take some time to think about and appreciate the darkness. Remind yourself that from darkness comes light, and that everything in our Universe is balanced. Think about any obstacles you have faced and overcome, and allow yourself to feel gratitude for

the lessons you have learned and the growth that came from those lessons as well.

5. As you observe the candle's flame, visualize its light spreading and illuminating the areas of your life where you seek renewal and growth.

6. Speak or silently express gratitude for the blessings and experiences of the past year.

7. Take one of the evergreen branches or wreaths in your hands, and feel its vibrancy, strength and resilience. It represents the continuity of life even in the freezing temperatures of winter.

8. Reflect on your own resilience and strength, acknowledging the hardships you have overcome.

9. Meditate on your desires and wishes for the coming year. Focus on personal development, growth, renewal, and inviting more light and joy into your life.

10. If you wish, recite a poem, chant, or affirmation that resonates with the themes of rebirth, renewal, and the return of light.

11. Conclude the ritual by extinguishing the candle, symbolizing the transformation from darkness to light.

12. Take some time to simply just "be" in the dark silence. Silence and darkness are actually two things that are quickly disappearing from our modern world, as most people stay glued to televisions, computers and phones until the wee morning hours. Thus, they miss out on the oh-so-important dark period of night, when the body can truly rest and renew itself. Be still, and appreciate this period of time.

13. Make sure you are bundled up in blankets or warm clothing, and spend a few moments outdoors, connecting with the winter night and embracing the power of darkness. It is from darkness, that all things are born.

When you go back inside, you will feel invigorated and prepared to welcome the longer days once they return.

## Summer Solstice Ritual: Celebrating the Sun's Return

During the Summer Solstice is when the sun finally reaches its peak, and we experience the longest days of the year, and shortest nights as well. It is a time that represents abundance, richness, birth, and growth, as nature is alive and thriving, and most crops are growing during this time as well. This ritual celebrates the power of the sun and invites blessings and abundance into your life.

Materials:

- Yellow or gold candle (representing the sun)

- Flowers, herbs, or plants associated with the summer season

- Matches or a lighter

Instructions:

1. Find a sunny space outside where you can comfortably perform the ritual, like a garden, park, or your backyard.

2. Set up your ritual space, and place a yellow or gold candle in the middle. Arrange flowers, herbs, or plants around it.

3. Light the candle, and focus on its flame, seeing it as representing the radiant, warm sun.

4. Breathe deeply, and use this moment to feel the warmth and energy of the sun on your skin and throughout your body, connecting you to its life-giving power.

5. Reflect on all the wonderful people and things in your life, feeling thankful for all the Universe has blessed you with.

6. Select a flower, herb, or plant from the arrangement and hold it in your hands. Breathe in its aroma, and appreciate its beau-

ty and vitality.

7. Meditate on your intentions for the season, focusing on growth, abundance, and manifesting your goals.

8. Visualize the sun's energy connecting with your intentions, empowering them, strengthening them so they grow.

9. If you want you can recite an affirmation, poem, or chant that resonates that relates to abundance, growth, or gratitude.

10. Offer a portion of the arrangement to nature by, for example, scattering flower petals in the air or on the ground, or placing herbs on the ground as an offering.

11. Conclude the ritual by thanking the sun for its energy and blessings.

12. After your ritual, enjoy some more time outdoors. Appreciate everything about this time of year, and enjoy the feel of the sun's light

upon your skin, warming you from the outside in.

## Spring Equinox Ritual

The Spring Equinox occurs during the time of year when daylight and nighttime are in perfect balance. It represents new beginnings, and the rebirth since nature is awakening once more, and birth in general as most animals are born during this time. This ritual celebrates the equilibrium of light and darkness and invites renewal and growth.

Materials:

- Green candle (representing new life and growth)

- Seeds or seedlings

- Soil or plant pot

- Matches or a lighter

Instructions:

1. Find an outdoor space or a windowsill where you can perform the ritual.

2. Set up your ritual space with the green candle placed in the center and the seeds or seedlings nearby.

3. Light the candle, focusing on its flame as a representation of new life and growth.

4. Take some time to just breathe deeply, and connect to the energy of Spring, feeling the rejuvenation and vitality of nature.

5. Reflect on the balance between light and darkness in this world, on the perfection that is nature, and feel a sense of gratitude wash over you.

6. Take one of the seeds or seedlings in your hands and visualize it as a beautiful symbol of your intentions for renewal and growth.

7. Plant the seed or seedling in the soil or pot, infusing it with your intentions for the sea-

son.

8. Meditate on your aspirations and goals, focusing on what you wish to manifest and nurture in your life.

9. If you wish, recite a poem, chant, or affirmation that resonates with the themes of new beginnings, balance, and growth.

10. Water the seed or seedling, visualizing your intentions taking root and blossoming.

11. End the ritual by expressing gratitude for the return of spring and the opportunities it brings.

12. Place the pot or container in a sunny spot, tending to the plant as it grows, symbolizing the nurturing of your intentions and goals.

**Autumn Equinox Ritual**

The Autumn Equinox occurs near the end of every September, when the sun is right above the equator, signaling the start of Fall in both hemispheres. During this time, the daylight and nighttime are 12 hours long all over the world, symbolizing a time of perfect balance and abundance since it is a time when many crops are harvested and stored for the coming winter months. This ritual is designed to celebrate the bountiful harvest and express gratitude for the gifts of nature.

Preparation:

- Choose a serene outdoor space, such as a garden or a park, where you can connect with the elements of nature.

- Dress in comfortable clothing that represents the colors of autumn - oranges, yellows, and deep reds.

Materials:

- a small bowl of water

- a candle (orange, yellow, or red)

- seasonal fruits and vegetables

- a journal and a pen

Instructions:

1. Opening the Circle:

- Stand in the middle of the space you've chosen, take a deep breath, then feel the earth beneath your feet. Imagine roots growing from your feet, planting you to the heart of Mother Earth.

- Hold your arms out to your sides, and form a circle with your body. When you do this, visualize a shining circle of light forming around you, creating a sacred and protected space for your ritual.

2. Honoring the Elements:
- Light the candle in the middle of your circle, that represents the fire element.

When you do this, say these words: "I honor the fire element, the sign that represents transformation, light and the warmth of the fireplace."

- Hold the bowl of water in your hands, acknowledging the water element water. Say: "I honor the water element, the source of life, cleansing and emotional flow."

- Take a moment to appreciate the air around you, symbolizing the air element. Then, whisper: "I honor the element of air, the breath of inspiration and communication."

- Finally, look to the earth beneath your feet and declare: "I honor the earth element, the foundation of abundance, grounding and growth."

3. Harvest of Gratitude:
   - Take the seasonal fruits and vegetables you gathered and put them on the ground in front of you. While you arrange them, think about all the blessings in your life and the abundance that surrounds you.

   - One by one, pick up each fruit or vegetable and express your gratitude for the gifts each represents. For example, you could say: "I am grateful for this apple, symbolizing the sweetness of life and the knowledge it brings."

- Feel free to speak your gratitude aloud or in your heart, nature will hear you regardless. Allow feelings of appreciation and thankfulness flow through you, filling you with joy and contentment.

4. Release and Renewal:
- Take your journal and pen, and find a quiet spot within the circle to sit down. Reflect on the past season and any emotions or experiences you wish to release.

- Write down all negative thoughts, fears, or burdens that no longer serve you. Acknowledge them as part of your journey of growth, but with the intention of letting them go.

- Once you've finished, rip the pages out of the journal and hold them in your hands. Visualize the weight of these heavy emotions leaving your body, making space for new growth and positive energy.

- With a deep breath, release the torn pages into the wind, watching them scatter and dissipate. As you do this, affirm: "I release what is no longer serving me, and I make room for new blessings to enter my life."

5. Closing the Circle:
  - Stand once again in the middle of your circle, facing each direction. Express your thankfulness to the elements for their presence and their help during your ritual.

  - Slowly lower your arms, feeling the circle of light gently dissolve around you. Know that you can recreate this sacred space whenever you need to connect with the energies of nature.

  - Blow out the candle, signifying the completion of your ritual.

After the ritual, take time to enjoy the sense of connection and gratitude. Take pride in yourself for honoring and celebrating the season of harvest of abundance, and released what no longer serves you. Carry this sense of renewal and gratitude with you while into the rest of the season.

The solstices and equinoxes provide powerful times throughout the year, where you can connect with nature in unique ways, appreciating the intelligence of the world. Nature always knows what we need. It provides us with time to rest, and time to be up, active and full of energy. As well, it provides us with the time to be balanced in both our rest and activity. Appreciate nature for this, and use these moments during the year to further connect to Earth, and work with the energies of each season.

Green witches do this through the performing of rituals that honor the start of each solstice. This naturally attunes us with the vibrations of our planet, creating powerful opportunities for positive changes in our lives.

Note: Allow the rituals in this book to be mere guidelines. You can always adjust them to better suit your intentions. Desires, belief systems, and the items you have on hand. It is my hope that these practices further enhance your relationship with magic and with nature.

# Chapter Eleven

# The Enchanting Power of Candle Magic

Green witchcraft has long revered candle magic as a powerful tool. For centuries, candles have illuminated paths toward transformation and connection with the unseen. Candle magic, also considered pyromancy, is an ancient art that taps into the deep symbolism of fire and its incredible power to bring forth passion, illumination, and transformation. For countless witches, fire embodies the spark of creation, igniting both physical and spiritual manifestations. By lighting candles, we bridge the earthly and ethereal realms, merging the power of nature with our intention to bring about meaningful shifts, blessings, and healing.

Candles themselves possess their own unique magical properties. Similarly, the flames and the shadows they cast have a particular enchanted essence too! As you explore this craft more deeply, you'll uncover a path to communicate with the Universe, seek guidance from higher realms, and help weave your intentions into reality.

In candle magic, the color of the candle you choose holds a lot of meaning and symbolism because it relates directly to specific elements of nature and goals. Each color aligns with certain emotions, properties, aspects of life, and elemental energies. This is why as green witches, we select the candle for our rituals and spellwork with great care and consideration, choosing the one that will best harmonize with our goals. Of course, as with all green witch magic, the most important factors in candle magic include your intentions and how you, personally, connect to the candle's meaning and energy.

Candle magic will often involve preparing the candle before burning it. This usually includes carving into the candle, anointing it with oil (and covering it in specially chosen herbs if you wish) or consecrating it. The ritual of lighting a candle represents a unique and sacred moment. As the flame flickers, we are able to reach out to powerful forces that can help us manifest our wishes - whether that be the Universe, our ancestors, deities or gods we connect with, or elemental beings. Through them, we can ask for anything from protection and healing, to gratitude, transformation and change. By aligning our intentions with the powerful flames created in candle magic, we are able to tap into the strong currents of energy that empower our spell work, aligning them with the forces of nature.

While you explore the practice of candle magic, you'll find that it serves as a vessel for your own self-discovery, personal growth, and deep connection to the natural world as a green witch.

## Candle Colors and Choosing the Right One For Your Spell Work

Colors have been used throughout the ages to communicate information and evoke emotions. In candle magic, the color of the candle is just as important as the intention behind it. Using colors intentionally in spell work infuses them with energies that help in the manifestation process. Different colors bring different properties that enable us to achieve a variety of purposes in our practice.

The most commonly used colors in candle magic are white, black, red, blue, green, yellow, and purple. Each color brings its own unique symbolism and energetic vibration that can be used to influence the outcome of any magical activity.

When creating a ritual with a specific goal in mind, it is best to incorporate one or more colors that correspond with your desired outcome to further assist in your spell's success.

Below is a brief description of the most common candle colors and their associated purposes, so you can choose your candle colors with intention and care each time you do spell work.

White: Represents purity, spirituality, and clarity. White candles are often used for purification, protection, and invoking divine guidance. They can also be used as a substitute for any other color when your desired color is not available.

Red: Symbolizes passion, love, and vitality. Red candles are used for spells related to romance, lust, sex magic, desire, strength, and courage. They can ignite passion, attract love, and increase energy and motivation.

Pink: Signifies love, compassion, and harmony. Pink candles are commonly used in spells related to self-love, friendship, emotional healing, and nurturing relationships. They promote gentle and unconditional love.

Orange: Represents creativity, success, happiness, and enthusiasm. Bright orange candles are often used to bring about feelings of confidence, hope, and motivation. They're believed to inspire creative energy and create enthusiasm in whatever task is being undertaken.

Yellow: Symbolizes intellect, communication, energy, and clarity. Yellow candles are used for spells related to learning, mental clarity, focus, and enhancing communication. They stimulate mental energy and improve concentration.

Green: Signifies growth, abundance, health, and fertility. Green candles are used for spells related to money, prosperity, wealth, luck, and physical healing. They bring about abundance, harmony, and the nurturing of new beginnings.

Blue: Represents peace, tranquility, and intuition. Blue candles are used for spells related to healing, inner peace, spiritual guidance, communicating with ancestors and those in higher realms. They promote calmness, serenity, and psychic awareness.

Purple: Symbolizes spirituality, wisdom, and transformation. Purple candles are often used in rituals when you wish to inspire the development of psychic powers, intuition, aid in spiritual growth, or work with your subconscious thoughts, as well as divination.

Black: Often used in banishing and releasing rituals to get rid of unwanted or undesired energies. Black candles are also used for spells related to breaking

hexes or curses, and protection against negativity. They symbolize the removal of obstacles and transformation.

Brown: Signifies stability, grounding, and practicality. Brown candles are used for spells related to home, peace, abundance, and connecting with the earth's energies. They provide grounding and enhance stability.

Gold: Symbolizes wealth, success, and achievement. Gold candles are used for spells related to financial abundance, career success, and personal achievement. They attract prosperity and success in various endeavors.

Silver: Represents intuition, reflection, and lunar energy. Silver candles are often used in spell work that assists one in sharpening their intuition, improving their psychic abilities, for more meaningful dreams. They promote spiritual insights and connection with the divine feminine.

These candle colors can be used individually or even altogether, depending on the spell you are casting and your specific intentions. It's important to trust your intuition when selecting colors, and as always, there really is no wrong way to be a green witch. You may have your own personal associations and preferences for the colors. Feel free to adapt them into your candle magic work if you wish.

## Beginning and Closing Candle Magic Rituals

Before you start a candle magic ritual, it's important to create a sacred space and set clear intentions. This section details a simple, step-by-step guide on how to begin and close candle magic ritual.

## Beginning the Candle Magic Ritual

Preparation: Find a peaceful place where you can be undisturbed while you perform your ritual. Next, choose a candle that resonates with you, some matches or a lighter, and any other items you will need for your ritual, like ritual oils, crystals or herbs.

Cleansing: Clear the energy of your space and tools. You can use methods like smudging with sage, spraying the area with Florida water, or visualizing white light cleansing the area.

Grounding and Centering: Never perform magic in a poor mood or mindset, as it can potentially affect our spell work in a negative way. Before beginning your spell, take a few moments to ground yourself and connect with your inner energy. Breathe deeply, focusing on your breath to release any tension or distractions.

Intentions: Set your intentions for this ritual. Clearly state what you desire to manifest or create, transform into or out of, achieve, or release. Visualize the outcome as if it has already happened. You can also write a petition - write your desired outcome on a piece of parchment paper - as a means of setting your intentions, and place it next to the candle.

Candle Selection: Choose a candle that aligns with your intention. Consider the color symbolism and energy associated with each candle color when making your decision.

Candle Preparation: Touch the candle and infuse it with your own energy and intentions. You can visualize your energy flowing into the candle or speak affirmations to charge it with your desires. This is also the time when you can anoint it with a ritual/drawing oil if you wish, and even rub herbs and flowers on it if you wish.

Lighting the Candle: Place the candle in a safe holder and light it with reverence. As you do, state your intention out loud or in your mind. Feel the flame's energy, and let yourself connect with its power.

Perform the Ritual: Focus and Visualization: Gaze into the flame of the candle, allowing your mind to focus solely on your intention. Visualize your desired outcome manifesting with as much clarity and detail as possible.

Affirmations or Incantations: Say affirmations or incantations that reinforce your intention. You can use pre-written ones or create your own on the spot. Repeat them with conviction and belief. Remember, it is all about your energy and intention.

Meditation and Energy Sending: Enter a meditative state and project your energy and intentions towards the flame. Visualize the energy flowing from your being to the candle, amplifying your intention.

**Closing a Candle Magic Ritual**

Gratitude: Express gratitude for the guidance and assistance you receive during the ritual. Thank the Universe, your deities, or any spiritual beings you work with for their presence and support.

Extinguishing the Candle: Once your ritual has ended, you may allow the candle to melt entirely, as you watch over it. Or, you can safely extinguish the candle flame by blowing it out, using a snuffer, or by using any candle extinguishing method you prefer. You can open a window at this point as well, allowing the smoke to flow out of your room, and into the air outside, inviting space in your house, and your life, for change.

Tip: Anytime you work with fire, it is always a good idea to have a glass of water somewhere nearby in case of fire. Fire accidents are rare, of course, but it is best to be safe. And as always, never leave a candle unattended.

Grounding and Release: Take a few moments to ground yourself by connecting with the earth. Imagine any excess energy dissipating into the ground, returning to its natural state.

Closing Words: End the ritual with your choice of closing words, or a phrase that

signifies the completion of your ritual. For example, you could say, "And so it is." "So mote it be." "It is done." Or, something as simple as "Blessed be."

Cleanse and Release: If desired, cleanse your space again to clear any residual energy. You can use methods like smudging, sound cleansing, or visualization.

As you continue on your journey as a green witch, it is so important that you believe in yourself and rely on your own intuition. Don't forget to practice with an open heart and tweak rituals so that they reflect what you feel is true. With time you will find a way to begin and end your candle magic rituals that feels the most powerful and genuine to you. Below are a few effective candle magic spells that are perfect for beginners.

## Success Spell

1. Choose an orange or gold candle.

2. Carve symbols or words representing success and achievement into the candle. For example, you can carve your intention into the candle, like "pass my exam." You can write an abbreviated version of your intention if needed. Use a pin or pen to easily carve your intent.

3. Next, feel free to dress your candle how you

choose. Personally, I dress my candles with a ritual oil like Anointing Oil, or an oil that promotes success and overcoming obstacles like Road Opener Oil. You can also use your own blend based on success-drawing herbs and oils. You can roll the candle in success-drawing herbs after this as well if you choose.

4. Concentrate on transferring your intentions into the candle as you dress it.

5. Next, light the candle and visualize yourself reaching your goals, experiencing your intentions, wishes, or desires, and embracing success.

6. In your mind or out loud, say:

*"With this flame, I draw success to me.*
*Strong is this flame, and powerful is the strength of my success.*

*I am now empowered to achieve greatness in*
___________*." (Whatever it is you desire.) And I de-*
*serve it. It is done."*

Or, you can create your own incantation, based on what feels good and true to you.

1. Sit for 5 - 10 minutes, picturing the success you wish to attract into your life.

2. Allow the candle to burn completely or extinguish it safely if needed.

The best days to complete success rituals are: Tuesdays and Sundays.

The best moon phase for success spell work is: Full moons.

**House Protection Spell**

1. Choose a black, blue, or white candle.

2. Carve symbols or words representing the protection of your home into the candle. For example, you can carve your intention into the candle, like "keep my home safe." You can write an abbreviated version of your inten-

tion if needed. Use a pin or pen to easily carve your intent.

3. Next, feel free to dress your candle how you choose. Personally, I dress my candles with a ritual oil like Anointing Oil, or an oil that promotes protection like Protection Oil. You can also use your own blend, based on success-drawing herbs and oils. You can roll the candle in protection-drawing herbs after this as well if you choose.

4. Concentrate on transferring your intentions into the candle as you dress it.

5. Next, light the candle and visualize yourself, your family and your home being safe and protected by a golden light that engulfs you all.

6. In your mind or out loud, say:

*"By the power of this flame, I draw protection to my home.*

*Only love, positivity, and harmony dwell within these walls. Cover this house, and all who dwell within it, in protective energy. It is done."*

Or, you can create your own incantation, based on what feels good and true to you.

1. Sit for 5 - 10 minutes picturing the protection you wish to attract into your life.

2. Allow the candle to burn completely or extinguish it safely if needed.

The best days to complete this ritual are: Saturday, Monday and Sunday.

The best moon phase for this spell work is: Full moon

## Attraction Spell

1. Choose a red, or pink candle.

2. Carve symbols or words representing the thing(s) you wish to attract into the candle. For example, you can carve your intention into the candle, like "A good friend" or "dream vacay to Maldives." You can write an

abbreviated version of your intention if needed. Use a pin or pen to easily carve your intent.

3. Next, feel free to dress your candle how you choose. Personally, I dress my candles with a ritual oil like Anointing Oil, or an oil that promotes attraction like Attraction Oil. You can also use your own blend, based on attraction-drawing herbs and oils. You can roll the candle in drawing herbs after this as well if you choose.

4. Concentrate on transferring your intentions into the candle as you dress it.

5. Next, light the candle and visualize yourself radiating magnetic energy, drawing in the desired people or opportunities.

6. In your mind or out loud, say:

*"By the power of this flame, I attract my desires. I desire to attract___________ into my life, because it is what I want and deserve. It is done."*

Or, you can create your own incantation, based on what feels good and true to you.

1. Sit for 5 - 10 minutes picturing the things or people you wish to attract into your life.

2. Allow the candle to burn completely or extinguish it safely if needed.

The best day to complete this ritual is: Friday.

The best moon phase for this spell work is: Waxing Moon.

**Scrying Spell**

1. Choose a purple or white candle.

2. Set up your scrying mirror or bowl filled with water on a table or altar in front of you.

3. Gaze into the mirror or water surface, focusing on a single point. Allow your vision to soften and become unfocused, entering a state of relaxed concentration.

4. Carve symbols or words representing the thing(s) you wish to attract into the candle.

For example, you can carve your intention into the candle, like "see beyond the veil." You can write an abbreviated version of your intention if needed. Use a pin or pen to easily carve your intent.

5. Next, feel free to dress your candle how you choose. Personally, I dress my candles with a ritual oil like Anointing Oil, or an oil that promotes divination like Visions Oil. You can also use your own blend, based on divination-drawing herbs and oils. You can roll the candle in drawing herbs after this as well if you choose.

6. Concentrate on transferring your intentions into the candle as you dress it.

7. Next, light the candle and visualize yourself seeing into the future, or seeing any hidden truths you wish to see.

8. In your mind or out loud, say:

*"With this candle's flame, I seek to see beyond the veil, to access hidden truths and receive divine guidance. I open myself to the visions that the Universe wishes to reveal. It is done."*

Or, you can create your own incantation, based on what feels good and true to you.

1. Sit for 10 - 15 minutes. Continue to gaze into the mirror or water, allowing your mind to enter a receptive state. Be open to any images, symbols, or messages that may arise in your mind's eye. Avoid straining or forcing the visions; let them come naturally and intuitively.

2. Allow the candle to burn completely or extinguish it safely if needed.

The best day to complete this ritual is: Wednesday. The best moon phase for this spell work is: Dark Moon or First Quarter Moon.

**Release Unhealthy Attachments Spell**

1. Choose a black or pink candle.

2. Grab a pen and a sheet of paper, as well as a

fire-safe bowl or cauldron.

3. Write down the attachments or connections you wish to release. Be specific and honest about what you want to let go of. As you write each attachment, visualize it leaving your energy field and being transferred to the paper.

4. Carve symbols or words representing the thing(s) you wish to release into the candle. For example, you can carve your intention into the candle, like "my toxic relationship." You can write an abbreviated version of your intention if needed. Use a pin or pen to easily carve your intent.

5. Next, feel free to dress your candle how you choose. You may choose to anoint your candle with essential oils that are known for their banishing properties, like black pepper oil. Or, you can also use your own blend.

6. Concentrate on transferring your intentions

into the candle as you dress it.

7. Next, light the candle and visualize the bond between you and whatever is you wish to let go of, burning away.

8. Hold the paper with your intentions above the black candle flame, allowing it to catch fire. Safely place the burning paper into the fire-safe bowl or cauldron. As the paper burns, imagine the unhealthy attachments disintegrating and transforming into smoke, releasing their hold on you.

9. In your mind or out loud, say the following 3 times, feeling the power and truth of these words:

*"I release what no longer serves me, setting myself free, Letting go of unhealthy attachments that bind me. With this flame's transformative light, I break free and soar to new heights. It is done."*

Or, you can create your own incantation based on what feels good and true to you.

10. Sit for 10 - 15 minutes. Close your eyes and visualize yourself surrounded by a vibrant, protective aura of light. See the smoke from the burning paper carrying away the negative energy and attachments, leaving you cleansed and liberated.

11. Allow the candle to burn completely or extinguish it safely if needed.

The best day to complete this ritual is: Saturday.

The best moon phase for this spell work is: Waning Moon.

**Honoring the Deceased Spell**

1. Choose a blue or purple candle.

2. Carve the person's name or initials into the candle.

3. A photograph of the deceased, or a memento.

4. Fresh flowers if you desire.

5. Gently arrange the photograph or memento and the bouquet of flowers around the blue candle, creating a sacred and inviting space.

6. Light the blue candle, symbolizing the illumination of the spirit and the connection to the afterlife, and picture the deceased in your mind as best you can. Ideally, it should be a happy memory or occasion.

7. Say aloud,

8. "_________ *(name) 's spirit burns brightly, just like this candle, while you live on in the afterlife.*"

9. Take a moment to gaze at the flame, focusing your mind and heart on your deceased relative. Think of the deceased at peace, and content.

10. At this time you may speak from the heart and address your departed relative if you wish, inviting their spirit to join you in this sacred space. Feel free to share your feelings, memories, and gratitude for the time you had together.

11. Speak or think "well wishes" and blessings to

send to your dearly departed. You may say something like: "May you find peace and eternal love as you journey into the realms beyond. May your spirit be free, and your soul be embraced by the light. You will forever be cherished and remembered with love."

12. Sit quietly for 5 -15 minutes, reflecting on the presence of your loved one, feeling their energy and love surrounding you. Allow any emotions to surface, honoring your feelings with compassion.

13. Pick up the flower(s) and hold them in your hands, infusing them with your love and intentions. Then, offer the bouquet to the photograph or memento as a symbol of your love and connection.

14. Allow the candle to burn completely or extinguish it safely if needed.

The best day to complete this ritual is: Wednesday.

The best moon phase for this spell work is: Full
Moon.

## Prosperity Spell

1. Choose a green or gold candle.

2. Carve symbols or words representing prosperity into the candle. For example, you can
   carve your intention into the candle, like "win
   the lottery," "a raise at work," "an abundant
   harvest," etc. You can write an abbreviated
   version of your intention if needed. Use a pin
   or pen to easily carve your intent.

3. Next, feel free to dress your candle how you
   choose. Personally, I dress my candles with
   a ritual oil like Anointing Oil, or an oil that
   promotes prosperity like Prosperity Oil. You
   can also use your own blend, based on success-drawing herbs and oils. You can rub the
   candle in prosperity-drawing herbs after this
   as well if you choose.

4. Next, if you have citrine, pyrite or any other

crystal that attracts wealth, place that next to your candle.

5. Concentrate on transferring your intentions into the candle as you dress it.

6. Next, light the candle and visualize prosperity flowing into your life, in whatever way you desire.

7. In your mind or out loud, say: *"By the power of this flame, I draw prosperity into my life.*

8. *Wealth, abundance, and riches flow into my life each day with ease and effortlessness. It is done."*

9. Or, you can create your own incantation, based on what feels good and true to you.

10. Sit for 5 - 10 minutes, picturing the prosperity you wish to attract into your life.

11. Allow the candle to burn completely or extinguish it safely if needed.

The best days to complete this ritual are: Wednesday.

The best moon phase for this spell work is: Full Moon.

**Overcome Fear Spell**

1. Choose a red or gold candle.

2. Carve symbols or words representing fearlessness into the candle. For example, you can carve your intention into the candle, like "overcome public speaking," "come out to my family," "start a new business," etc. You can write an abbreviated version of your intention if needed. Use a pin or pen to easily carve your intent.

3. Next, feel free to dress your candle how you choose. You can coat your candle in oils that promote self-empowerment and bravery, like eucalyptus oil, frankincense oil, and lavender oil. You can rub the candle in bravery-drawing herbs after this as well if you choose.

4. Concentrate on transferring your intentions into the candle as you dress it.

5. Next, light the candle and visualize your fears leaving your body.

6. In your mind or out loud, say:

7. *"By the power of this flame, I draw bravery into my body.*

8. *Fear, uncertainty and anxiety has no place within me anymore. As sure as this fire burns, so too does my certainty that I can achieve anything I want and more with no fear! It is done."*

9. Or, you can create your own incantation, based on what feels good and true to you.

10. Sit for 5 - 10 minutes, picturing the fear that is holding you back, now leaving your body and your life for good.

11. Allow the candle to burn completely or extinguish it safely if needed.

The best day to complete this ritual is: Tuesday.

The best moon phase for this spell work is: Waxing Moon.

## Healing Spell

1. Choose a green candle.

2. Carve symbols or words representing health into the candle. For example, you can carve your intention into the candle, like "healthy weight," "good blood pressure," "pain-free," "healthy gut," etc. You can write an abbreviated version of your intention if needed. Use a pin or pen to easily carve your intent.

3. Next, feel free to dress your candle how you choose. You can coat your candle in oils that promote health, like Healing Oil. You can rub the candle in health-drawing herbs after this as well if you choose.

4. Concentrate on transferring your intentions into the candle as you dress it.

5. Next, light the candle and visualize your health being restored and your body feeling perfect!

6. In your mind or out loud, say:

7. *"By the power of this flame, I command health to be restored to my*

8. *body. Only health, vitality, and energy is allowed to dwell within me.*

9. *As sure as this fire burns, so too does my health. It is done."*

10. Or, you can create your own incantation, based on what feels good and true to you.

11. Sit for 5 - 10 minutes visualizing your health being restored and feeling how wonderful and revitalized you are because of that. Feel a sense of gratitude for your health's return because health is actually the human body's natural state.

12. Allow the candle to burn completely or ex-

tinguish it safely if needed.

The best day to complete this ritual is: Sunday.

The best moon phase for this spell work is: Waxing Moon.

**Increase Your Power Spell**

1. Choose a purple candle.

2. Carve symbols or words representing power into the candle. For example, you can carve your intention into the candle, like "clairvoyance," "intuitive," "telepathy," "prophetic dreams," etc. You can write an abbreviated version of your intention if needed. Use a pin or pen to easily carve your intent.

3. Next, feel free to dress your candle how you choose. You can coat your candle in oils that promote divination like Visions Oil. Or you can create your own blend. You can rub the candle in divination-drawing herbs after this as well if you choose.

4. Concentrate on transferring your intentions into the candle as you dress it.

5. Next, light the candle and visualize your fears leaving your body.

6. In your mind or out loud, say:

7. *"Each day, the power within me grows as steadily as this flame.*

8. *Each day, I see evidence of power increasing. And the more*

9. *evidence I see, the more it grows. The more I use my power, the*

10. *stronger I become. And so, it is."*

11. Or, you can create your own incantation, based on what feels good and true to you.

12. Sit for 5 - 10 minutes visualizing your hidden gifts awakening and your current gifts strengthening. Feel the power circulating throughout your body, energizing you in

every way. Recognize that you are, in fact, superhuman.

13. Allow the candle to burn completely or extinguish it safely if needed.

The best day to complete this ritual is: Monday.

The best moon phase for this spell work is: First Quarter Moon.

## Moon Phases and Spells

Did you know that each moon phase correlates to certain types of spell work? It's true. Green witches don't just revere the moon for its mysterious allure. The moon possesses energies that are strongest during certain moon phases, and we can work with those energies to amplify the results of our spellwork. Here is a quick breakdown of these phases and the spells that benefit the most when performed during that time.

Full Moon: The moon is at its full power during this time. Apply the intense energy to any spell you choose, but especially: balance, cleansing, charging, divination, healing, clarity, love magic, water magic, protection, dreams, communicating (with ancestors, gods, etc. our gods and ancestors), psychic abilities, self-development, and more! Many witches charge crystals under this light.

Waning Moon: Best time to release that which no longer serves you, break bad habits and addiction, toxicity in life and relationships, illness or addiction, letting go, for wisdom (Waning Gibbous). A great time to perform spells that lessen things like unhappiness, poor health or poverty. Spells that undo or break curse and bindings, inspire forgiveness and cleansing. Also an optimal time to perform destructive magic - hexes, curses, jinxes etc.

New Moon / Dark Moon: A time to start over, and create new beginnings. A great time to perform shadow work and past life regression as well. Great for spells that concern: new love, new friendships, new opportunities, protection, banishing, letting go of the past, clearing bad energy from your life, cleansing, removing curses and hexes, peace, justice, and fertility. Also, an optimal time to perform destructive magic - hexes, jinxes, curses, etc. and an excellent time to break them as well.

Waxing Moon: The moon phase where the moon looks especially big and bright. A great time for growth in your life. An ideal time to perform constructive magic for good health, joy, prosperity, attraction, beauty, creativity, strength, courage, wealth, luck, success, self-esteem, love, friendship, motivation, abundance, etc.

Now that you have a sense of how candle magic works, the significance of the candle colors, and even the best moon phases for performing certain spells, you can tweak the spells and incantations in this chapter to suit your own needs. Meaning that, yes, you can easily craft your own candle spells! Guidelines like moon phases, candle colors, examples of incantations, etc. are all wonderful things to know as you learn more about green witchcraft, but always remember there is no "correct" way to perform magic. So long as you focus on your intent and you act based on your intuition, you will see results. And, results speak for themselves.

# Chapter Twelve

# Conclusion: Embracing the Magic Within You

You've reached the end of this book, but it is my hope that this enchanting introduction to green witchcraft is just the beginning of your journey! Through these pages, you have cultivated self-knowledge and self-discovery by learning to connect with and harness the Earth's energies. May you always take the lessons, profound wisdom and magic that lies within nature, and recognize that they are not separate from your own body and spirit.

For green witches, witchcraft is more than a ritual or a practice; it is our way of life. As displayed in this book, it is possible for us humans to connect deeply with the world around us, and to understand how to best work with the rhythms of nature's changing seasons. And, it is important for us to do so.

For instance, with your newfound knowledge of herbalism, you've learned how to tap into and harness the medicinal and magical properties of plants to manifest your greatest desires, and to transform your life and the lives of others. This is achieved through various means like blending ritual oils, brewing teas, sewing dream pillows, making brooms, mixing Florida water, and consuming magical meals with intention. In the art of candle magic, you learned the secrets of how and why fire is vital to green witchcraft. You also learned how to use a candle, and the sacred flame, to infuse your desires with fire energy, helping them materialize with speed and ease.

Through the information in this book, you have been introduced to many sacred green witch rituals that will aid you in cultivating a deep sense of connection with the Universe, recognizing the magic that lies both within and around you.

As you continue to walk this path, remember that green witchcraft is unique to each green witch, and an ever-evolving practice. Again, there is no right or wrong way to perform this magic. As long as you focus on your intentions when performing magic, and you are seeing results, you are doing great. Ultimately, *you* are the creator of your magical path. Embrace your intuition, trust your inner wisdom, and never shy away from exploring the realms of the mystical, occult and the unknown.

From now on, move forward confidently, knowing that the magic you possess is a force of love, healing, and transformation infused with nature's energy! As you continue to weave the threads of your destiny, let your heart guide you to places where the wild and magical energies of the Earth intertwine.

Now, young green witch, get out there and embrace this magical practice. Let it guide, inspire, and fill your life with wonder, fulfillment, joy and enchantment. May you walk the path of the green witch with grace, wisdom, and the knowledge that you are a force of nature, connected to the vast circle of life.

So, don't hold yourself back. The world is waiting for the magic that only you can bring.

B        l        e        s        s        e        d    be.

# Chapter Thirteen

# Author's Note

Congratulations for beginning your amazing journey into the world of green witchcraft. It is my hope that this book has provided you with valuable insights, practical guidance, and a deeper connection to nature's magic. As you continue to explore the path of the green witch, remember that the real magic lies, not in an herb, nor a crystal, food or tea, but within you. You have, and have always had, the ability to create radically positive changes in your life. Green witchcraft, like all witchcraft, is a life long path. May yours be always magical, interesting and rewarding.

And do keep in mind: When you "work with Nature" you are actually working with yourself, because you are literally a part of Nature. There is no difference because separation between you and the world around you is just an illusion. When you realize this, and take it to heart, you will be in flabbergasted at how much more powerful your magic becomes, and how easy it is to manifest the wishes and intentions you desire into your life.

If you've found inspiration within these pages and wish to continue your magical exploration, I invite you to join my mailing list. By subscribing, you'll receive exclusive updates, tips, and special offers on future books, handcrafted witchcraft supplies that enhance your practice and your journey towards spiritual and physical growth and well-being. (From ritual oils and spell blends to artisanal teas, tarot cards, sustainably sourced crystals, and more) We do not believe in spamming our readers and supporters. You can join here: https://mailchi.mp/4535e93ef5dc/join-our-readers-list

Visit our website to discover a treasure trove of unique tools that amplify your magical endeavors. Each item is lovingly crafted with intention, harnessing the energy of nature to empower your spells, rituals, and daily practices. Together, let's embrace green witch magic and paint our intentions onto the canvas of the universe.

Thank you for being part of our vibrant community, and may your path be illuminated with the light of wisdom and wonder.

Blessed be, AwakenedYou Family